SHAM PEARLS FOR REAL SWINE

Sham Pearls for Real Swine

Beyond the Cultural Dark Age — A Quest for Renaissance

FRANKY·SCHAEFFER

Wolgemuth & Hyatt, Publishers, Inc.
Brentwood, Tennessee

Wolgemuth & Hyatt, Publishers, Inc.
1749 Mallory Lane, Suite 110
Brentwood, Tennessee 37027

Library of Congress Cataloging-in-Publication Data

Schaeffer, Franky.
    Sham pearls for real swine / Franky Schaeffer. — 2nd ed.
        p. cm.
    ISBN 1-56121-089-7
    1. Christianity and the arts. I. Title.
BR115.A8S32 1990
261.5'7—dc20   90-31541
                                                                                    CIP

For my patient daughter Jessica

CONTENTS

ACKNOWLEDGMENTS

First, I would like to thank a number of people who specifically encouraged me to write this book: John Cox, John Whitehead, Thom Howard, Steven Hawley, Paul and Kristina McGuire, my wife, Genie Schaeffer, and my mother, Edith Schaeffer.

Second, I would like to thank Michael Hyatt for his wonderful encouragement throughout this project. His support has been unusual in its kindness and understanding. I would also like to acknowledge the friendship and support of Robert Wolgemuth as he stood behind me in the writing of this book. Russ Sorensen, my editor, and Susan Kirby, who copyedited my book, were both tremendously helpful and pleasant to work with. Thank you!

A "thank you" is also in order to my children, Jessica, Dani (her husband), Francis, and John (and, again, to my wife Genie), for all the love, patience, and affection with which I am undeservedly surrounded.

Thank you, Paul and Kristina McGuire for providing a home away from home for me in Hollywood. And thank you to Jim and Judy Buchfuehfer for your long, loyal friendship. Thank you, Lori Ambacher and Genie Schaeffer for typing my many handwritten drafts (more than a dozen) of this book when I needed them done rather than when it was convenient to you both. I would also like to thank Norman Podhoretz, editor of *Commentary* magazine, for so generously allowing me to quote at length from several articles published in *Commentary* (published monthly by the American Jewish Committee, 165 East 56th St., New York, NY 10022), as well as to the other publishers and authors quoted in this book.

Franky Schaeffer
February 1990

PROLOGUE

All you have to do is write one true sentence.

ERNEST HEMINGWAY

Sir Winston Churchill coined the phrase "sham pearls for real swine" in reference to the British public school (private prep school to Americans) he attended. He said of the teaching there that it was a place "where sham pearls were fed to real swine." Unfortunately, the same can be said of a great deal of teaching in the Christian church concerning the arts, media, and our culture in general.

Perhaps I have, by using this title, handed my critics, "the carping censures of the world" (Shakespeare, *Richard III*), an easy turn of phrase with which to dismiss the book on the basis of the title being an apt description of my book's contents! If so, well and good. I aim to please and what better way to do this than to hand one's head to a critic on a platter with, as Bertie Wooster would say, "watercress all 'round it!"

Since writing my first book, *Addicted to Mediocrity*, in 1980, I have been on some strange adventures. For one thing, I have changed careers from that of a documentary filmmaker to that of a feature film director and screenwriter.

The movie industry is a tough, strange, and often lonely business. As a Christian working in the arts, I have naturally looked to other Christians for encouragement, yet there are problems within Christendom concerning its understanding of the arts. Middle America and its religious expression, evangelical fundamentalism, is often unsympathetic to the arts and to cultural endeavor. Where, then, is the Christian pursuing a career in the arts to turn for inspiration, help, and advice?

As for the arts, what are they for? What do they "do"? Mainly, as far as many Christians are concerned, they scandalize, perplex, and anger. Strange priorities rule the sensibilities of some Christians. Four-

1

letter words used in films outrage the brethren, yet routine lies in the church hardly cause comment. Nudity on the stage, screen, or canvas arouses fundamentalists to fury, yet a carnival atmosphere of debauched materialism reigns unchallenged in much of the church.

The values of middle America are replacing the biblical absolutes of the historic church. If it were thinkable, God would be blamed by some Christians for creating too much—too much lusty flesh, too many pretty women, too much natural diversity. If Shakespeare were understood today, his plays, the glorious pinnacle of Christian morality expressed through drama, would be banned as "unsuitable" by much of the modern fundamentalist church. If Leonardo da Vinci and Michelangelo were working as our contemporaries, they would face hostility from some quarters in the church. The Bible itself, if read as a book and not as a spiritual devotional mantra, would be rejected as a profane oddity, filled with sexual and violent images.

Some Christians have said that they want to "restore and reclaim America," to return to an earlier innocence, to "go back." But, we may ask, back to what? The 1950s? What other age beyond our own of anesthetized, plastic propriety could accommodate us? What past leaders would meet our standards of piety? Luther? We would find him vulgar. Shakespeare? Filthy. Bach? Secular. Verdi? Catholic. Joan of Arc? Insane. Winston Churchill? A drunken warmonger. George Washington? A reactionary chauvinist. Jesus of Nazareth? Rude, sexist, offensive, and inscrutable. All of these would be too complicated, too real, too human for the "nice," the timid, the shallow, the ignorant—the church.

The dedicated Christian pursuing a career in the arts or media is caught between a hammer and an anvil—the hammer of *closed-minded* secularism and the anvil of *closed-minded* fundamentalist Christianity. Please don't misunderstand me. I believe in the fundamentals of the historic Christian Faith, and I do not have an axe to grind with evangelical fundamentalism. I object only to the closed-mindedness and the anti-cultural baggage that today is often characteristic of the Protestant community. The Christian in the arts has a narrow and precarious road to walk. I attempt to walk that road in my profession as a movie director and screenwriter; I proceed with many a stumble. I hope this book will perhaps serve others engaged in the arts, and other walks of life, who share that elusive path with me. This book necessarily draws lessons from my film-making experiences which I trust will be applicable to my readers in their own lives and work. I hope others will find that events in my life will relate to their own and that my conclusions, drawn from experience, study, and long reflection, will help them.

Now that this book is being reprinted in its paperback edition, I have availed myself of the opportunity to re-order some of the chapters, add a little material, cut some, and re-edit the remainder. Thus, to those who, for some inexplicable reason, might re-read this edition after having first read the hard cover, yes, I have made some changes, and no, you do not need to get your eyes examined.

My intention in writing this book is to help generate a robust discussion of the problems and ideas I set forth in this volume. My intention is *not* to set myself up as an "expert" of some sort or to present my book as the only opinion or the last word on the subject. My voice is only one among many.

As G. K. Chesterton remarked in the introduction to his book, *St. Thomas Aquinas,* "I can only express the hope, and indeed the confidence, that those that regard me as the heretic will hardly blame me for expressing my own conviction."

1

OUR CHILDREN AND OURSELVES

Who has not felt how sadly sweet
The dream of home, the dream of home,
Steals o'er the heart, too soon to fleet,
When for o'er sea or land we roam?

SIR THOMAS MORE, *The Dream of Home*

G rowing up in an evangelical Christian community in Switzerland (what would have been called a commune in the 1960s), L'Abri Fellowship, I absorbed the idea that it was normal to have an interest in and love of the arts. My late father, Francis Schaeffer, introduced me to the arts, including film. He encouraged me to organize film festivals for the L'Abri community. (This sometimes presented problems for students visiting from evangelical-fundamentalist colleges who had signed pledges promising not to, among a host of other forbidden things, go to movies!) L'Abri Fellowship would hire a local theater and rent movies to watch and discuss. *Satyricon, The Pawnbroker*, and Bergman's various pictures were some of the many films I remember watching. The reason we watched them was not only to learn from them but also because we enjoyed them. L'Abri also organized art festivals and art weeks—times of poetry readings, music, performances, art exhibits, as well as film screenings.

When I was fourteen years old, my father took me out of school for three weeks and traveled with me to Florence, Italy. I recall walking through the Uffizzi Gallery, standing in awe before the works of Botticelli, walking into the Academia and looking at Michelangelo's *David* for the first time, and having Renaissance art history from the early works of Giotto and Masaccio up to the late High Renaissance of Raphael knowledgeably explained to me as we tramped through the galleries and churches.

Because of my mother's and father's positive attitude toward the arts and humanities, I took it for granted that enjoyment of art, beauty, and history was naturally part of the Christian life. I thought that to be interested in Roman history or in a film about the Roman Empire's decline (like Fellini's *Satyricon*) was natural and good. I did not then appreciate the fact that I was living in an oasis.

At sixteen, with my father's blessing and encouragement, I took my first paying job related to media. I worked on a light show for the Led Zeppelin *rock* band at the Montreux jazz-rock festival. My father invited the rest of the light show crew and me up to L'Abri to put on a light show in the chapel one evening (to recorded music; we couldn't afford the band).

While working at the festival, I remember noticing Jimmy Page, the Zeppelin's lead guitarist, reading Dad's book *Escape from Reason* backstage before a show. He had been given the book by Eric Clapton, of The Cream, who in turn had received it from a British rock critic who had become converted to Christianity at L'Abri. (Dad had an early interest in and appreciation of acid rock, and often listened to it and discussed it and other contemporary music with his students and me at L'Abri.)

As a child growing up in L'Abri, I never knew that there were "R"-rated movies. I only knew there were well-made films and poorly made films. I never knew nudity portrayed in art and film was "evil." I never knew that four-letter words invalidated someone's book or film, and made it "unacceptable," (though I was taught not to use profanity in polite conversation). I thank God for my ignorance during those formative years. When my father expressed himself at all on the subject of narrow fundamentalist and evangelical attitudes toward art and culture, it was to bewail the lack of vision and harsh treatment of artists, not the "evils" of the "world."

I was taught by my father and mother to judge artwork on its artistic merits and that the moral rightness or wrongness of things, such as nudity, violence, or profane language in the arts, depended on their context, the honesty of the work, its quality, and the subject matter.

As a result, it never occurred to me to confuse what was right, as far as personal moral behavior went, and what was appropriate to portray in the arts and media. Violence was part of life; therefore, I was given to understand, it should be portrayed in art forms when necessary to the story. Some people used "bad language" in life. They, too, had stories honestly worth exploring through the arts and film—stories that could not be told if the syntax and phrases of profanity were eliminated from the characters' vocabulary.

It was my parents' encouragement, through their own interest in the arts and their practical financial help, that led me to seriously pursue my own career, first in painting, then later as a movie director and screenwriter. To be a director, painter, or writer seemed a very natural career to choose for someone raised in a family that loved art, books, and movies, as well as the people who made them. For years my parents generously purchased art supplies for my use in my painting, sculpting, and woodcuts. My father always found the time and money to help me in my early, experimental super 8 mm films. He sat for hours in my studio workshop at my film-editing bench criticizing my early film efforts and special effects' experiments. I remember him helping me one afternoon mix up a batch of "blood" mix for a "suicide" I was filming using his secretary as my "actress" and "stunt woman." She survived, though it took her two weeks to get the red paint stains out of her hair!

From an early age, my shelves were bursting with books about every subject imaginable. My mother spent hours reading aloud to her children. My dad and I often went to movies together. It was a good, full, and culturally rich life that I led, perched on a hillside in that small, obscure, Christian community.

My father and my mother raised their children to be unafraid of ideas and unafraid of being intellectually challenged, quite an achievement for my mother who came from a very pietistic background. She was raised in a China Inland Mission home by parents who washed her mouth out with soap for using a *minced oath*. Minced oaths were even the subject of an earnest tract my missionary grandfather wrote. (A *minced oath* is any word used as an expletive that even *sounds* as if it *might* be bad. *Darn*, for instance, *might* be mistaken for *damn*. Get the soap!)

My mother made a series of conscious decisions to reevaluate what was and was *not* important for her children to learn about moral essentials. God bless her and my father for all the fundamentalist baggage they chose to leave behind so that their children would not have to carry it into that hard oblivion that awaits so many of the faithful.

Only later in life did I begin to meet the types of Christians who took it for granted that you were supposed to protect your children from "The World." Often this protection appeared to be an attempt to hide from reality and, above all, to not be challenged to answer your children's questions.

However, aside from the clear absolutes of Scripture, there *were* other taboos in my family. My parents protected me as best they could, not from art or hard questions, but from mediocrity. That was why we had so few contemporary evangelical or fundamentalist books in the house. That was why we had no television set—thank God! That was why my parents never played contemporary Christian music of the gospel variety, let alone trash pop. I grew up thinking that the label of "sacred music" referred to Bach, Buxtehude, Mahalia Jackson, and Handel. For me, contemporary music was Miles Davis' jazz or the poignant singing of Billie Holiday. My father's favorite "contemporary music" was Bob Dylan songs like "Route 66" and later the Beatles' "Sergeant Pepper's," which he listened to endlessly and discussed avidly and sang along with in his terrible off-key voice upon occasion.

In recent years, it has amazed me to hear my father referred to—in some quarters, by some people who should know better—as a "fundamentalist" (with the anticultural content which that label now deservedly denotes). One can believe in the fundamentals of the Christian faith without carrying the cultural know-nothing baggage of fundamentalism. I remember my dad as the man who took me to Fellini's movie *La Dolce Vita* and discussed it with me over a cup of coffee while lending me twenty centime pieces to feed the jukebox so we could listen to The Mothers of Invention's latest hit, *Brown Shoes Don't Make It*. I remember sitting on the steps of the Duomo in Florence at two in the morning and discussing the design competition which resulted in Ghiberti creating the panels for the east door of the Baptistery, the *Doors of Paradise* as Michelangelo later dubbed them. Was forty years too long to spend on one artwork? Judging by Ghiberti's results, we decided it wasn't!

My father never protected his children from ideas, from art, from intellectual challenge and stimulation, or from contrary thinking, even anti-Christian, anti-biblical art, thought, and culture. Believing that Christianity was truth, he welcomed honest questions. If this was "fundamentalism," then let there be more of it!

I was raised in a family that read books, went to movies, talked, and did *not* watch television. It is an abiding irony that many of the evangelicals and fundamentalists who welcomed, often misreading, parts of my late father's critique of certain aspects of secular culture, never understood, let alone shared, his basic love of the artworks, books, and movies he was critiquing. My father spent his life feeling uncomfortable with the evangelical establishment, even as they made his books into best-sellers. "Life," as he was apt to say, "is strange."

Today

Now, years later, married and with my own children (as I write, ages twenty, seventeen, and ten), I have come full circle to stand in the place of a parent. My wife and I have done everything we can to pass on the treasure of both open-minded, sensible inquiry, and orthodox historic Christianity to our three children. In raising children there are no guaranteed results. Yet there are ways of improving their chances of suc-

---

"The problem is that the very leaders of the church that people look to for guidance are themselves caught in and totally encultured by the tasteless supermarket wasteland that is now middle America."

---

ceeding in life as full human beings. There are also ways of almost guaranteeing bad results. At least we as parents can try to avoid that.

Having children has forced my wife and me to think a lot about education. In America today, there seems to be an unintentional collusion between church and the state. This has produced ugliness and mediocrity in American culture and daily life. The state has failed to educate through its public schools, and the church has not met the challenge.

Secular v. Christian

The state's schools cannot educate because many of the people who run and teach in them no longer believe in their own culture, the West, or in moral absolutes informed by Jewish-Christian teaching. The church and its schools are governed by people who may believe in absolutes in a theoretical way, but have been so compromised by tasteless, artless, mundane, and plastic middle America that they have nothing fresh, interesting, or profound to teach their students beyond pietistic platitudes and second-rate "basics." In many cases, in the "religious" schools and the "secular" schools, there is no commitment to Western cultural and historical knowledge (beyond the most minimal American civics) and barely token interest in European Western history, culture, and art. In the main, our schools in America now inhabit a cultural wasteland of rootless anti-knowledge.

Thus, at the very moment when our bankrupt state, "secular" education system is producing tasteless, uneducated, barely literate young people, who graduate to become empty, lumpish adults, or worse, the church and its schools can do no better than to add a few pious teachings and Bible verses to the general chaos of ignorance and entertainment masquerading as education. We are now, therefore, paying the dreadful price for a twentieth-century brand of evangelical-fundamentalist Christianity that has regarded culture, history, worship, art, and learning as "unspiritual," thus unimportant.

Today, most evangelical and fundamentalist Christian education is either of the Victorian Sunday school variety or simply secular non-education with a few Bible verses thrown in, along with some tub-thumping, nationalistic "patriotism" for good measure. The blind are leading the blind. Ignorant, pietistic teachers are passing on a-cultural learning to the children of ignorant parents. "Secular" or "Christian," our population all watch the same television programs; this is their only remaining "cultural" bond it would seem.

Perhaps there is less respect for learning today than in the gloomiest period of the so-called Dark Ages, during which there was at least a high degree of *reverence* for learning even by those who possessed very little themselves.

Just Coping

Today, many Christian families are so bogged down in attempting to cope with divorce, adultery, and all the other immoral plagues of our time, that Christian teaching directed at the family seems to be more of a Christianized psychological counseling service than real education that advances truth and human aspirations. *How to Cope with This or That* could be the generic catch-all title of most evangelical-fundamentalist Christian books. The problem is that the very leaders of the church that people

---

"The pagan, non-Christian culture is crying out for aesthetic and cultural leadership, and all we Christians offer is plastic pablum, formula 'gospel.'"

---

look to for guidance are themselves caught in and totally enculturated by the tasteless supermarket wasteland that is now middle America.

The pagan, non-Christian culture is crying out for aesthetic and cultural leadership, and all we Christians offer is plastic pablum, formula "gospel." "Christian" education is aiding and abetting the cultural decline of the West. The church unwittingly joins hands with the graffiti-spraying gangs of the inner cities, just as the Visigoths joined hands with the Vandals in the pillage of the Roman Empire. We do not even know what we are throwing away.

Television programming, materialism, the a-historical, anti-Western, anti-education of most evangelical fundamentalist and non-Christian schools alike—these form the vortex into which the sensibilities of our culture are inexorably sucked. Culture, education, art, and intellectual risk are abandoned in favor of easy materialism and lazy lives spent in light amusements. Disney's Epcot Center is a representatively horrible idea of "culture as we now understand it." Steven Spielberg's trivialization of the supernatural is now our idea of "spirituality." Scholarship and appreciating the arts is dismissed as irrelevant by "right thinking" political propagandists masquerading as intellectuals. Middle Americana, its valueless values and its niceties, are often all that remain to us of our glorious past.

Christian educators congratulate themselves because some statistics show that they teach more children to read than their even less effective secular counterparts. To read what? To write what? To speak what? To see what? To listen to what? To discuss what? To change what? To challenge what? To become what? To love what?

Given the indifferent results of the Christian schools in providing a real cultural alternative to anti-Western secular education (a fact that is glaringly apparent to anyone like me who has traveled around the country speaking at the many evangelical colleges that dot the landscape), the Christian parent must face the reality that it is imperative to find that rare thing, a good school, and enroll one's children. We parents must also face the fact that, even if our children are in a good school, their primary source of moral and cultural education will be in the home.

Whether a school is Christian, secular, or a home school is not the point. Good education is what we must pursue for our children. And since most Christian and secular schools, from kindergarten through college, are today so lacking in a Jewish-Christian-Western worldview, we parents must compensate by becoming educators ourselves.

This means we have to spend a great deal of time with our children reading, discussing, and exploring. *It also means that we cannot be lazy in our own continuing education and reading.* We need to have a well-formed view of Western culture, history, and the arts ourselves if we are to help our children. If we are samples of most Christian homes and contemporary schools, to become educated ourselves will take a real effort of the will. By reading, studying, watching, and discussing, we will have to engage in our own courses of study. Today in our anti-cultural, a-historical society, we are all deprived and ignorant to one degree or another. We have been cheated of our inheritance. We are *all* in the dark. And our efforts to find the light will be hard and clumsy. But we must persevere.

At various stages in our family life, my children have been home-schooled, attended an evangelical Christian primary school, and a secular, liberal high school. What my wife and I have pursued for our children is good teaching and a love of learning and culture, not ideological or theological purity on the part of our children's teachers.

"In our family, we have found it necessary to make sure that organized activities do not diminish precious family time."

All knowledge comes from one source—God. Truth, good teaching, and culture are where you find them. Truth about a subject taught by non-Christians is better than falsehood taught us by Christians, or vice versa. It is a question of truth—as in medicine, it is a question of good surgery, not "Christian" surgery. Better a competent, atheist cardiologist who will help you survive your heart attack, than a well-meaning, bumbling, and incompetent Christian doctor who will pray over your corpse once he's killed you!

That even good schools are so often imperfect is all the more reason to make the home a place of comfort and creativity. It seems to me that the importance of all education, especially formal schooling, should be kept in proportion to what makes up the rest of life. When school activities conflict with important family time, we take our children out of school, even if it means short-term academic setbacks. There are more important things than school, and schools, even good ones, will never compensate for mediocre or broken homes.

Activities

In our family, we have found it necessary to make sure that organized activities do not diminish precious family time. A long evening meal at the end of every day during which the day's ideas and events are discussed, reading aloud, a day off together—these are untouchable, sacred familial institutions to us.

To have time together, a family has to have the discipline to say no to many activities. Children who are allowed to treat dinner as a "pit stop" on the way back to other activities will never be around long enough for you to get to know, teach, or enjoy. Parents who constantly treat their children as burdens on their time, while they rush off to do Important Adult Things, will have children who do, in fact, become burdens.

In our family, we try to minimize irrelevant social interruptions. My wife and I have seen our children and our marriage as the priority in our lives. Whoever came up with the idea of "quality time" with children as a replacement for spending a lot of time with them was a fool.

I have often slipped out of meetings with my producer or agent, saying that I had "an important appointment to get to." The appointment was to take my wife and children to a museum or a movie, then lounge around a Chinese restaurant afterward discussing it. You have to beg, borrow, and steal family time from a world bent on distracting you from the most important things in life.

Religion

You can ask a child to memorize one Bible verse too many. You can share one little platitude as an answer to a real question once too often. There *is* a straw that breaks the camel's back. If you are teaching obedience to Christ and enjoying the ancient traditions of the historic church and its rich Christian liturgy, the Eucharist, the meaning of the sacraments and worship, teaching the value of Western culture, its art, its thought, studying its history, discussing today's movies and politics, looking at the world of nature and nature's God (and *not* watching television), your children *will* be naturally surrounded by the fruit of historic Christianity and its thought. They will still have to make their own choices about what they believe to be true, but they will have something positive by which to judge the claims of the aggressively secularist world. And who knows, they may even be able to think rationally in this fundamentally irrational age!

A child's interest in the gospel can be harmed by well-meaning parents. Bible verses taught out of context, devotional time as a pietistic duty, endless "churchianity" rather than actual liturgical worship—these are sterile and counterproductive activities when forced on children.

Many Christian parents are amazed that their children do not follow their footsteps in the faith. Often they have only themselves to blame. There is such a thing as too much of a good thing. So much of the church today is shallow and rootless, cut off from the faith of our fathers, sound doctrine, sacraments, liturgy, teaching, and practice, that it is no wonder many children will abandon it as they grow up. Overabundant, fraudulent piety without content is no replacement for truth and the sacraments, and young people know or feel this instinctively.

Tasteless, glitzy, evangelical, "charismatic," and fundamentalist activities are no substitute for genuine sacramental worship, obedience to Christ, and holy tradition, any more than the kind of gospel quartets that appear on

> **"So much of the church today is shallow and rootless, cut off from the faith of our fathers, sound doctrine, sacraments, liturgy, teaching, and practice, that it is no wonder many children will abandon it as they grow up."**

thousands of church platforms every Sunday are any substitute for authentic music.

Today, the heart of the gospel has been cut out of much so-called Christian worship. And the children who rebel against this fraud are often right in doing so. They are not rejecting the historic truth of Christianity but rather the silliness, harshness, and finally the lies of pietistic Protestant Christianity. Deprived of the glories of the ancient changeless traditions of the church, these children have never seen the gospel in action, beyond calls to personal religiosity and make-it-up-as-you-go-along "worship" as entertainment.

Some pastors, either bored, misled, or trying to work out their own inner problems, lead their congregations on strange journeys. Inner healing, wholeness, renewal, signs and wonders, liberal theology, or other fads sweep the church. The church dilutes the gospel and the Holy Spirit's power when it embraces other things that replace Christ and His historical apostolic church. Pop psychology and Christianity merge uncomfortably in many so-called inner healing ministries. The church loses sight of Christ as He becomes obscured by a myriad of social programs and activities or doctrinal emphasis foreign to the gospel and the ancient traditions and liturgies of the Orthodox, ageless church. The church ceases to be *the* church when it becomes, for instance, a psychological counseling service advocating simplistic techniques on how to be "whole," "happy," or "fulfilled."

In many churches today, Christ is presented as simply a superfriend to help us with our psychological problems. The hard edges of truth and the demands the real historic Christ makes are abandoned in favor of what amounts to religious group therapy. The Body and the Blood are abandoned in favor of the psychiatrist's couch. It is the "me," the ego, that such religion serves, not the living God.

People involved in such ecclesiastical diversions begin to look inward. They become selfish, professionally and permanently wounded and needy; "hurting" becomes a badge of self-centered honor. People dredge up their pasts to find out who or what was responsible for their problems. Church becomes a source of drama and entertainment to fill the empty spaces that sacramental worship and life itself should fill when lived in daily obedience to Christ and in the enjoyment of other people, culture, and natural beauty.

Because of the failure of the secular religions, including psychology, to genuinely meet people's needs as sinners, the irony is that the nonbelieving world now turns increasingly to "religion," through things like the New Age Movement, to help heal people's problems caused by sin. Yet pitifully, the church itself turns to psychological counseling, under many guises, to heal what *is* in fact sin that only Christ can forgive and cure.

Pietism and psycho-babble are perfect companions. The one maintains the outward niceties and virtues of middle America, while the other allows us to wallow in selfish, narcissistic contemplation. Sin and judgment are forgotten as endless sermons on "love" soothe our frayed nerves. Salvation is reduced to an alternative to Valium. Being "whole" or happy is seen as more important than being virtuous, let alone repentant.

By my observation of the many distressed parents I have known, if you want to guarantee that your children finally abandon the faith, then bring them up in an overwrought church that is off on some inward-looking, self-conscious, anti-historical tangent. Any tangent, beyond the historic church's basic orthodox function, will do: inner healing, psycho-

---

"In many churches today, Christ is presented as simply a superfriend to help us with our psychological problems."

---

babble, charismatic gifts (of the circus variety), feminism, social work, antinuclear pacifism, harsh reformed doctrine, pietism, tough-minded fundamentalism, smarmy, self-satisfied, evangelical "churchianity," even an overindulgent sacramentalism in which the sacraments begin to take on the magical aura of a talisman—this last being the final refuge of ex-fundamentalist Episcopalian rascals who love the liturgy more for its aesthetic qualities than for its true meaning. The list of diversions is as endless as are the dollars to be raised from the flock, and the victims as numerous as the misguided, unstable people who are looking for personal "meaning" rather than for truth.

When Christ, the Holy Spirit, and the ancient rites of the historic church are "improved upon," beware! When any fad is followed that creates a little circle of special, in-the-know, "anointed" Christians, separated from the apostolic church, speaking their own enlightened dialect—be it charismatic, psychological, or aesthetic and liturgical—the whole purpose of fellowship is thwarted. If we begin to associate only with people in the church who are like us, or "good for us spiritually," we are on the road to a cult, however enlightened its beginnings.

Perhaps T. S. Eliot summed it up when he sardonically observed, "Certain saints found the following of Christ very hard, but modern methods have facilitated everything."

Television

Television is a blood-sucking parasite. Even if all the programming was of universally high caliber, the point stands. It is foolish to spend too much time in any passive pursuit which bombards the mind with a numbing series of unrelated imagery that cuts off rational communication with other people.

There are some serious scholars who have even argued that there is a direct link between the amount of television we watch and the abysmal educational standards we in our country have come to accept as "inevitable." According to them, the visual stimuli of television and the disjointed avalanche of images, that often have little or no logical sequence, actually have affected, even changed, the very way people think. People raised in an environment of television's kaleidoscopic whirlwind of imagery will not be able to think in as linear and rational a manner as people trained to think, read, and question have been in the past. Neil Postman, in his book *Amusing Ourselves to Death*, brilliantly argues that television has changed our society for the worst. Others have also made a similar case—for instance, Marshall McLuhan, Jerry Mander, Jerome Bruner, and Jack Goody.

An acute problem that television exacerbates is the loss of the sense of immediate community—of family, church, town, even state and country—as it gives the viewer the instant reality of "news" that is usually accompanied by flimsy, if any, analysis. After being ceaselessly pounded by emotive but unrelated images, people then feel that they are informed but remain ignorant of any real content, background, or history surrounding the events they have "seen." They thus can feel "in touch" with the world without actually being in touch with anything other than visual impressions. In the same way that the image culture replaced the book culture, emotional feelings are now replacing logic as a means of judging reality. This is a poor substitute for real study, contemplation, and reflection.

But the very lie that *is* television is hard to see since the sheer volume of programs offered seems to indicate that there is more substance there than there is. Like Shakespeare's idiot full of sound of fury signifying nothing, television leaves us empty.

One can watch endless "live" reports from some hot-breaking news story, yet gain less from the hours of television images than from a thirty-minute reading of a comprehensive explanation and history of the same event in some good journal of current affairs, such as *Commentary* or *First Things.* Yet the lure and lazy ease of television's accessibility is more than many people seem able to resist, for themselves or their children.

Just because our culture seems to be moving away from rational discourse to the imagery of emotionalism, and just because some churches themselves seem to be joining in this wholesale abandonment of logic and rationality as they embrace emotionalism, does not mean that we or our children are condemned to follow the trend. The off switch on the television set and the simple action of reading widely and consistently to ourselves and our children are the beginnings of a quiet revolution for truth we can undertake in our homes.

Perhaps a few enlightened, educated believing Christians who read while others watch will be the last of a dwindling band of people who can think in linear, rational terms.

Reading Aloud

Reading aloud to our children, by the hour, has been one of the most positive things that we have done together as a family. *Huckleberry Finn, Oliver Twist, The Bible, Animal Farm,* P. G. Wodehouse, *Emille and the Detectives, A Hitchhiker's Guide to the Galaxy, The Lord of the Rings, The Odyssey, The Chronicles of Narnia, A Brave New World, The Lord of the Flies, Wind in the Willows, Alice in Wonderland, The Adventures of Sherlock Holmes, King Solomon's Mines, Babar the Elephant, The Medici, The Last Lion, Modern Times, Art of the West,* articles from *Commentary* and *First Things,* Beatrix Potter's books, history, and art history—these only begin to cover the long list of books we have read together aloud. Biographies and many other books read aloud, literally hundreds of them, have provided an anchor for our family times and a means by which to introduce our children to their culture. Children are surprisingly attentive when raised in a family that reads aloud. Children understand far more than most people seem to think they do. We have read hundreds of books aloud in our family; many of them were passed on to me from my mother, who read hundreds of books to my sisters and me when we were children.

My mother is not alone in extolling the virtues of reading. Neil Postman writes:

From Erasmus in the sixteenth century to Elizabeth Eisenstein in the twentieth, almost every scholar who has grappled with the question of what reading does to one's habits of mind has concluded that the process encourages rationality; that the sequential, propositional character of the written word fosters what Walter Ong calls the "analytic management of knowledge." To engage the written word means to follow a line of thought, which requires considerable powers of classifying, inference-making and reasoning. It means to uncover lies, confusions, and overgeneralizations, to detect abuses of logic and common sense. It also means to weigh ideas, to compare and contrast assertions, to connect one generalization to another. (*Amusing Ourselves to Death* [New York: Viking Penguin, 1985], 51)

Children who love books, stories, ideas, drama, and debate come alive as human beings. Children who want to reread *Alice in Wonderland* are in the end profoundly more human than children who want nothing more than to watch one more mind-freezing hour of badly animated cartoons. Children who are read aloud to in the end will read to themselves for pleasure.

For me as a parent, some of the most satisfying moments with my children have been the times when I have seen the fruit of my wife's and my own reading labors. For instance, I was reading aloud recently to my ten-year-old son from a book about art history. In one chapter on Greek art was an illustration of a Greek vase depicting a scene drawn from mythology. My boy's excitement was no less than my own as he pointed to the picture and said, "I *know* what that is!" He identified the story depicted on the vase because we had been reading Greek mythology together some time before, and he had learned the story. He had also seen similar vases at the fine collection of the Getty Museum in Los Angeles. He was beginning to "connect the dots" for himself.

History

An understanding of history through reading, especially the reading of biographies, is absolutely essential to understanding who we are and what Greek-Roman, Jewish-Christian teaching and art has created in our Western culture.

Children who grow up and leave their home unacquainted with their cultural inheritance, which came from Byzantine Christian culture then from Western European sources and includes such colorful and inspiring people as Abraham, St. Constantine, Irenaeus of Lyon, St. Ignatius, Winston Churchill, Douglas MacArthur, Charlemagne, Queen Elizabeth I, Lorenzo de' Medici, Homer, Leonardo da Vinci, and many other figures of art, political, or religious history are poorer than they need be. People without knowledge and appreciation of their history are impoverished, rootless, and open to every lie told them about their nation, civilization, and the world. As American parents raising our families in the United States, it is important to remember that the *West* is our heritage and that its history and culture encompass far more than America's short existence. What happened in Byzantium or in Florence during the Renaissance is, for instance, just as vital to us today and to our children as what happened recently in American history. St. Augustine, Dante, and Charlotte Brontë are just as much our *founding fathers* (mothers) as are Jefferson and Washington.

Music

Performing music, learning an instrument, reading biographies of the composers, listening to and attending concerts, and learning to read music all draw out the best in children and their parents.

The Byzantine and Latin West has produced unrivaled glories in the field of music. Christians who waste their time listening to most so-called contemporary Christian music, contemporary sacred music, and songs of praise—the staple of so much evangelical Christian radio—are like the starved victims of a concentration camp subsisting *voluntarily* on moldy potatoes when a feast is set before them after liberation! Certainly there are serious Christians engaged in making good contemporary music, but those who limit themselves to contemporary popular "Christian music" seem to be unaware that the horizons are so much broader.

The classical music of the West belongs to *us,* up to and including jazz, the classical music of the twentieth century. Thus, children raised in a musical environment of Christianized ditties are being cheated of their aesthetic and spiritual inheritance.

Bach, Mozart, Vivaldi, Debussy, Verdi, Billie Holiday, B. B. King—the list of composers and performers who created our musical inheritance is almost endless. The music of the West *is* Christian culture. Sadly, there are Christian families who fail to raise their children with an understanding of this fact—this triumph of artistic truth with its power to lift the human spirit above the urban sprawl.

Not all the good music is from the past. A great deal of modern jazz with its roots in the joyful celebration of New Orleans jazz and black spirituals, some country and bluegrass music, a number of contemporary film scores, and some rock and roll (Hendrix, Clapton, etc.) come to mind as artists well worth listening to, studying, and enjoying.

The Home

Children can and should pass from childhood to young adulthood. While many normal young adults do tend to act rather imbecilic at some point in their development (as I certainly did), nevertheless, the concept of out-of-control "teenager-hood," as we know it today, is an invention of our failed, middle class, television saturated society. It is a concept used as an excuse, as if it were a force of nature beyond our control, to explain parents' and educators' failures to discipline children and introduce them to the world of ideas. "Teenager-hood" is a handy excuse to use when explaining the resulting chaos caused by these "children" as they are let loose on society by parents who have failed to be good stewards of God's most precious gift, their children.

Parents

If we want interesting, obedient children, we as parents have to be interesting ourselves and obedient to Christ. We have to read, watch, and listen. If we want children who are interested in culture, then our children must see our interest. If we want the truth about Jesus Christ to be interesting to our child, then, our own lives, which we claim are based on the truth, must compete with the interest, diversity, beauty, artistic creativity, and intelligence often found in the non-Christian community. If we want children who are fully human, then we must set our sights and expectations higher for them than the world does. We can do more for them than giving up the educational moral high ground and teaching them to use condoms! If these objectives seem hard to achieve, they are.

We may have to rearrange our own lives, change jobs, lower our standard of living, make less money, or move our residence to accommodate the breadth of life and learning that will help our families and ourselves be fully human. However, there is no more pleasant cross to bear than that of giving up the materialism that has come to dominate our time, and instead, putting our children ahead of our ambitions.

My wife and I have, for our children's sake, made practical choices that have often been in some ways sacrificial. In our case, for instance

"There is no more pleasant cross to bear than that of giving up the materialism that has come to dominate our time, and instead, putting our children ahead of our ambitions."

in one not-so-sacrificial example, I have chosen to live in a small New England town, not in Los Angeles or Hollywood. The fact that I do not live in the heart of the movie industry means that my career, such as it is, has suffered. I make much less money. I am not often in the "right place at the right time" to make "deals." In our particular case, the school situation, the large garden for the children to play in, the friends, and the Orthodox church that God has given us have all added up to good reasons to make less money. My wife and I have enjoyed a rich existence together *because* she has not worked outside the home but instead has chosen to raise a family. She and I have found genuine fulfillment in the home—a home in which her well-read, articulate, luminous presence is like a bright, clear light.

Beauty

Tastes vary, and anyone who ventures to discuss taste, let alone criticize bad taste, is running the risk of sounding pompous. Yet it should be self-evident that a home filled with books, art, music, solid old furniture or well-designed modern furniture, gardening tools, or just plain nothing at all but clean white walls, is preferable to, for lack of a better word, the all-too-familiar *kitsch* of middle Americana.

A stranger to our culture might be pardoned if he assumed that bad taste was the distinguishing mark of the evangelical and fundamentalist Christian "culture," as circumcision is the mark of the Jew!

Visual aesthetics do make a difference in our daily lives. We can either deaden and damage our aesthetic senses or stimulate them by what we see and hear. We are not alone as we make aesthetic choices; we are not starting over. We have our Christian inheritance and its traditions to study and to inspire us. We can examine what others, perhaps better informed aesthetically than we, found pleasing to the eye and ear, and emulate them.

There are, of course, many rewarding avenues of exploration (beyond our scope to examine here) open to us in helping our children discover the rich generosity of a full life. The appreciation of art museums, sports, nature study, the history and meaning of liturgical worship and Orthodox tradition, and languages come to mind as things that should be an integral part of our lives. All of these will increase our interest in our fellow men and women and point toward our creative God who is, after all, Lord of all we are, see, and do.

2

FISH IN BOILING WATER

My angel—his name is Freedom.
Choose him to be your king;
He shall cut pathways east and west,
And fend you with his wing.

EMERSON, *Boston Hymn*

I am not the only Christian to have taken a hard, critical look at Christians' recent efforts in the arts and media. For instance, my late father (Francis Schaeffer) had a great interest in the subject. While looking through some of his old correspondence recently, I found a letter dated August 19, 1982. Dad was writing to a Mr. French of Ann Arbor, Michigan, to advise him regarding a conflict with the elders of his church who were refusing to take a stand on sanctity-of-life issues. Yet, somewhat surprisingly, Dad's comments began by focusing on another issue: the arts. He wrote:

> What you are up against in your church there is all too tragically common in many of our Bible-believing churches. As you know, I speak of *the false view of pietism and spirituality*. . . . There is no doubt in my mind that biblically it is just that—it is a false view of spirituality. The price for this, as for all things less than God calls us to, has been overwhelmingly costly, first in individual lives. We have had so many young people come here to L'Abri who become Christians and then [return to a] . . . church holding this false view of spirituality . . . [that] told them that their art, music, or poetry . . . is subspiritual. Through the years literally hundreds of them have come here destroyed and wiped out. Happily, for many of them we have seen them set free and they are now creating again.

It is interesting to note that my father began a letter on why a church and its elders would be silent on a major medical ethical moral issue, abortion, by stating his views on the tragedy of the lack of understanding of the arts by many Christians, and equating the two problems.

I have learned to my sorrow that people in the Christian church are often far from sharing my father's enlightened appreciation of the arts, let alone supporting those of us pursuing artistic careers.

Plastic Churches

Most contemporary American church buildings are symbolically ugly, accurately reflecting the taste of pastor and people alike. In Los Angeles, Atlanta, and Dallas, for example, one finds a number of so-called superchurches—churches with five thousand to ten thousand members. These churches house congregations with the money, power, and means to build contemporary Chartres cathedrals, if they had the vision. The profound ugliness of these churches is not the result of budget priorities. These buildings are expensive; studied ugliness does not come cheap. Many of these church buildings seem to express the same sense of aesthetics as that of the living-room/kitchen set from the old "Dick Van Dyke Show." They constitute an assault on the senses: a nightmare of red velvet and prefab ceiling "tile," StainWare carpet in pastel shades from hell and the Easter Bunny, a Mt. Everest of canned sweet corn and lime JELL-O.

Distorted echoes of a now-pacified Christianity ring out in an electronic clarion call to middle America. These churches are the elevator music of religion, the counseling rooms in which the latest psycho-babble is used to assuage the anxieties of the pre- and post-mid-life crises, menopausal congregation. They provide childcare facilities to assist families in staying apart. In Christian bookstores, greeting cards and wall plaques decorated with pious sayings compete for space with the latest cassette tape wisdom of the local Protestant "pope" of the superchurch ministry outreach, worldwide international evangelism, counseling/suicide prevention hotline, daycare, elementary school, high school, senior citizen center, Bible school, fund raising, youth center, parking lot ghetto. If these churches were food, they would have a shelf life of one hundred years—all sugar and preservatives, the two basic evangelical-fundamentalist intellectual food groups. They are giant cash registers in which sham pearls are fed to the enlightened who in turn excrete money to feed the machine. Here, the creative person has as much chance of thriving as the plastic plants do in the artificial light of the "sanctuary."

"[Contemporary] churches are the elevator music of religion, the counseling rooms in which the latest psycho-babble is used to assuage the anxieties of the pre- and post-mid-life crises, menopausal congregation."

For in such "churches" liturgical and sacramental worship has long since been abandoned. Replaced by entertainment for the saints, true worship has withered and in its wake aesthetics of all kinds have also perished.

Art

The arts ask hard questions. Art incinerates polyester/velvet dreams of inner healing and cheap grace. Art hurts, slaps, and defines. Art is interested in truth: in bad words spoken by bad people, in good words spoken by good people, in sin and goodness, in life, sex, birth, color, texture, death, love, hate, nature, man, religion, music, God, fire, water, and air. Art tears down, builds up, and redefines. Art is uncomfortable. Good art (which, among other things, means truth-telling art) is good in itself, *even when it is about bad things.* All art is in a sense an icon—an image of man who is created in God's image; a testament to the fact that the physical world has been redeemed by the Incarnation of Christ.

Good art expresses an interest in everything. Art, like the Bible, is not defined by one period of history. Art explores immorality and immortality. There are no taboo subjects for good art, any more than there is taboo news for newspapers, because art is unafraid of the truth. Art, like Christ, comes to sinners in an imperfect world. People who imagine themselves to be perfect do not like art. The middle-class church, living in a cocoon of false expectations, resents people who wield sharp razor blades or worse, disturb their sleep. Art is fleshly yet eternal. Art is human. Art is a mirror to the world. Art is the bridge between flesh and soul. "Art is science in the flesh," as Jean Cocteau wrote in *Le Rappel a l'Ordre*.

Because art destroys a false sense of security, it is looked on with suspicion, even perceived as an enemy by the middle class and its spokespersons in the church, who, through ignorance, subdue artists and discourage talent. "Do not offend your brother" is a Bible verse often misused to intimidate the artist in the same way as "turn the other cheek" is sometimes taken out of biblical context to justify "Christian" pacifism. There is a Bible verse handily available for every tyrannical cause, to be exploited by those who use the Bible as an ideological • weapon.

Literature

The Bible

Only by giving the Bible a devotional spin when we read it, by taking isolated verses out of context and ignoring the raw whole, by filtering and interpreting, do we "civilize" it. Civilized, the Bible has become a devotional prop of middle-class values instead of being the rude challenge to false propriety it actually is. The Bible is a dangerous, un-civilized, abrasive, raw, complicated, aggressive, scandalous, and offensive book. The Bible is the literature of God, and literature, as every book burner knows, is dangerous. The Bible is the drama of God; it is God's *Hamlet, Canterbury Tales,* and *Wuthering Heights.* The Bible is, among other things, about God, men, women, sex, lies, truth, sin, goodness, fornication, adultery, murder, childbearing, virgins, whores, blasphemy, prayer, wine, food, history, nature, poetry, rape, love, salvation, damnation, temptation, and angels. Today the Bible is widely venerated but rarely read. If the Bible were a film, it would be R-rated in some parts, X-rated in others. The Bible is not middle class. The Bible is not "nice." The Bible's tone is closer to that of the late Lenny Bruce than to that of the hushed piety of some ministers.

In some centuries, the church did not allow the common people to read the Bible. Now by spiritualizing it and taming it through devotional and theological interpretations, the church once again muzzles the book

---

"The Bible is a dangerous, uncivilized, abrasive, raw, complicated, aggressive, scandalous, and offensive book. The Bible is the literature of God."

---

in a "damage control" exercise. We now study the Bible but through a filter of piety that castrates its virility.

When the unfiltered power of biblical understanding has occasionally broken into the open, there have been cultural results. The powerful, biblically based Dutch paintings of Rembrandt and Vermeer serve as examples with their reflections of raw, genuine life. For instance, there are the exquisite nude paintings of Rembrandt's wife. We see portraits of friends, simple scenes from everyday life, as in Vermeer's *Girl Interrupted at Her Music,* in which common events of life are portrayed as luminous events. Odd, earthy moments are depicted as well; an old man and woman urinating by the roadside is captured in a Rembrandt etching. Life as a whole—the good, the bad, the indifferent, the odd, the funny—was painted by great artists who *were* believing Christians.

The stunningly beautiful mosaics of the third and fourth centuries in Ravenna, Italy, tell the tale of a deep, Orthodox Byzantine spirituality, brilliantly executed by loving hands. These works were made by artists who loved Jesus and looked to Him for salvation, who understood the cultural and artistic basis that Christian tradition gives to those in the arts.

Shakespeare

The painters, scholars, sculptors, and philosophers were not the only Christians who shaped our culture. Consider Shakespeare, the truth-seeker, the glory of the English-speaking peoples; Shakespeare, who created both that saint of chaste Christianity, Desdemona in *Othello,* and the ribald sexual humor and double meanings in *The Comedy of Errors;* Shakespeare, who gives us truth about life—life theatrically painted as lovingly, humorously, and truly as it ever will be. His was drama based on a sense of Christian morality, drama that today the ignorant, *a-cultural* protestant church would reject as *un-Christian* if it were reproduced in language we understood. *Un-Christian* because it does not reflect middle-class nicety and propriety. Yet in Shakespeare's life and writing, we see a testimony to the Christian faith and its cultural fruit. S. Schoenbaum, Franklyn Bliss Snyder Professor of English at Northwestern University and one of the most world-renowned Elizabethan scholars, writes of Shakespeare's Christian faith:

> Inculcated from the formative years of early childhood, the Bible and Book of Common Prayer . . . profoundly nourished Shakespeare's imagination. One learned biblical scholar, ranging through all the works . . . has identified quotations from, or references to, forty-two books of the Bible—eighteen each from the Old and New Testaments, and six from the Apocrypha. Scarcely a phrase from the first three chapters of Genesis escapes allusion in the plays. Job and Ecclesiastes were favorite books, but Cain left an especially powerful impression—Shakespeare refers to him at least twenty-five times. . . . Shakespeare's range of religious reference is not limited to the Bible. Sometimes he quotes Scripture by way of the Prayer Book. (From *William Shakespeare, A Documentary Life* [New York: Oxford University Press, 1975], 48-49)

Music

The breast of the church once also nurtured composers: Vivaldi, Mozart, Bach, Corelli, Albinoni, Handel, Verdi, to name just a few of hundreds. Many looked to the historic Jesus for their personal salvation; all worked in an atmosphere informed by Christian sensibilities. Christian truth, set many free to be the people they were created to be, to use the talents God gave them. The traditions of the church provided a moral framework which was the foundation of the great artistic achievements of Western culture, just as the framework of historic Christianity had informed the glorious artistic achievements in the Byzantine empire with its enamel works, liturgies, music, sculpture, jewelry, icons, and learned literary works.

The Dilemma

Yet today it seems truth expressed through the arts is at war with a false spirituality which pervades many churches. The servants of hypocrisy, found in abundance in the bosom of Christianized middle America, are not the friends of the arts.

Loneliness is a constant reality for Christians who seriously pursue an artistic career. We are caught on the horns of a miserable dilemma. On the one hand is the church; on the other is the larger world and its art community. The nonbelieving art community, be it in the field of painting, theater, writing, film, music, or dance, has little interest in those who would express orthodox Christian themes through their personal lives or their artworks. Yet most churches are no better; they have lost vital contact with art and culture and have even lost the cultural vocabulary to discuss art and the humanities, let alone encourage artists.

To better understand the dilemma faced by believing Christian artists, let us look at an analogous example. There are some African languages in which the future tense does not exist. (This linguistically reflects a theological belief in animistic fatalism.) Thus, for some tribes there is no way to discuss the future as we would understand it; what the ancestors did of old will be done again tomorrow. An African health worker who is confronted by such linguistic barriers to progress and tries to explain some future project, for instance changing a tribal custom in a way that will be of benefit hygienically, has a nearly impossible task. The words do not exist with which to describe a different future reality.

Many Christians in the arts face the same frustrating dilemma today. Because Christian contact with the arts has recently been so minimal and hostile, the artist cannot discuss his or her art with fellow believers in a way that will be understood. There is no common vocabulary.

The contemporary, middle-class church is living in a historical vacuum. The church is largely unaware of its own cultural past. With each
successive split and realignment within Protestantism, the church has
moved further away from its cultural inheritance. Within the Catholic
community, liberal theology and leftist politics have served to under-
mine its traditional commitment to the arts as the church has focused on
"political relevance" at the expense of spirituality and culture. Today,
with only a few exceptions, the church and church-related educational
institutions are not centers of interest in history of any kind, let alone the
history of art and culture. Nor are church institutions mounting a coher-
ent defense of Western culture against the anti-Western tide that is
sweeping the intellectual world.

The Great Divorce

The modern protestant-evangelical church is now thoroughly divorced
from its historic culture. While claiming to wish to "reach mankind," it
often fails because our culture *cannot* be reached from outside by out-
siders who do not even bother to learn the cultural language. Ironically,
because the church does not understand or even care about its own cultural artistic history, it does not understand its own finest, nonreligious
creation: Western culture. In this way, the protestant church is like a bad
parent who has abandoned its child. Robert Nisbet writes, "Western philosophy can be declared a series of footnotes on St. Augustine" (*History
of the Idea of Progress* [New York: Basic Books, 1980], 71). Nisbet
expresses a sentiment as a secular scholar that many Christians seem to
have forgotten: Western art and culture *are* Christian at their roots.

Believing Christians who work in the secular art community are not
only misunderstood by the church because of its ignorance about art, but
worse, are often rejected as "unspiritual" for concentrating on a
"worldly" pursuit instead of a "spiritual" or "humanitarian" one.

The modern church, when it sees a contemporary Christian's artwork, has little knowledge and negligible historical perspective with
which to judge it. It simply passes judgments based on current middle-
class ideas of what is "appropriate" or in "good taste" or what represents
ideological "right thinking."

Since today's middle American ideas of virtue are not those that
have historically inspired great art, there is a conflict between members

of the middle-class church and those who would be serious artists. For instance, current middle American, post-Victorian ideas of propriety hold that all nudity in art is "bad." Yet an artist who does not draw the nude figure cannot learn the traditional, accumulated skills of thousands of years of figurative Western art history—much of it church-supported, Christian art history—and pays a severe artistic price for such willful ignorance.

However, there are much deeper problems preventing the church from having a positive cultural influence. The church, both "liberal" and "conservative," is now living in a historical vacuum; it wants instant results when it seeks to change culture. The idea of a historical unfolding such as the Renaissance, that took four hundred years to mature, is totally foreign to the modern church that measures everything in TV "sound bite" increments.

Hans Rookmaaker, the late Dutch evangelical Christian art historian and head of the art history department at the Free University of Amsterdam, has explained that any significant influence believing Christians in our time might have in the arts would take *generations*. This idea does not play well to a church that wants its problems solved in one weekend retreat, wants the world converted in one evangelistic rally, or sees its mission as encouraging the redistribution of wealth between people to achieve instant "justice."

Middle America, politically left and right, in cutting itself off from a historical understanding of Western culture, has become an aesthetic nightmare. Thus, even when it comes to personal taste, individuals in the church are rarely sympathetic to good art. Middle America knows what it likes, and it's awful! This problem is not confined to protestant America. A recent book with a self-explanatory title, *Why Catholics Can't Sing,* explores the degeneration of liturgies in the Roman Catholic Church as "liturgists" have tried to accommodate the lowest common denominator in the "folk masses."

In this tasteless world, the artist is condemned for being "secular" by the church and is ostracized by his or her nonbelieving contemporaries for being foolishly "religious." In the smooth world that is Christianity in America today, how many people can feel the poignancy of Emily Dickinson's immortal line, "I died for beauty" or the depth of the artistic struggle described by Graham Greene in what he called "the despair of never getting anything right"?

Visual, as well as literary, expression is foreign to most of today's church. This lack of understanding is exacerbated by the fact that few leaders in the church come from a background that would give them any particular knowledge of, or sympathy for, the visual arts. As a result, we have a legion of theologically trained but artistically boorish Christians who are the leaders of evangelical fundamentalist and Roman Catholic Christianity.

Some Christians have called for more involvement in the culture by the church. However, usually when Christian leaders have called for a Christian presence in the arts or media, what they have actually had in mind is the making of gospel propaganda or so-called family entertainment that embodies what they are pleased to call "traditional values." More often than not, what these offerings turn out to be is middle-class pablum that will offend no one, cause no one to think, mean nothing, and leave its audience as comfortable and mindless as before they were fleetingly entertained by it. In other words, the "traditional values" turn out to be the values of the 1950s middle America, not the far more robust traditions of historic Christianity. What most Christians seem to crave when they call for a Christian presence in the arts is a return to middle American sentimentality, the kind of sentimentality that confuses virtue with niceness. This is a long way from the expressionist realism we find in the Bible itself, a long way from a concept of truth that traditional Orthodox, Jesuit, *and* even Calvinist scholarship once would have defended as the basis for a self-confident Western civilization.

Overreaction to Secularization

Christians are threatened by the aggressive secularism of our time, often with good reason. Unfortunately, our reaction to disturbing trends of secularization has led to the creation of defensive Christian ghettos in education, the church, and the mind. Our own confused reactions in this respect are not much different than those of Christians in the fourteenth century, a similarly convulsed period of history, of which the late historian Barbara Tuchman wrote:

> Times of anxiety nourish belief in conspiracies of evil, which in the
> 14th century were seen as the work of persons or groups with access

to diabolical aid. . . . The Church was on the defensive, torn apart by
the schism, challenged in authority and doctrine by aggressive movements of dissent, beset by cries for reform. Like the ordinary man, it
felt surrounded by malevolent forces. (*A Distant Mirror* [New York:
Knopf, 1978], 514-515)

No better description could be written with reference to the attitudes
of many Christians in our own day to the secularist onslaught. In the
most unfortunate reaction possible, many Christians find false security

---

**"When Christian leaders have called
for a Christian presence in the arts or
media, what they have actually had in
mind is the making of gospel
propaganda or so-called family
entertainment. . . . What these offerings
turn out to be is middle-class pablum
that will offend no one, cause no one
to think, mean nothing, and leave its
audience as comfortable and mindless
as before they were fleetingly
entertained by it."**

---

through collective ignorance and deny rather than affirm, run rather than
shape, endlessly say no rather than present good alternatives. The Christian who is serious about being an artist occupies, in this reactionary
ghetto, a place as comfortable as that of a live fish placed in boiling
water.

The church is ugly when it begins to defend itself rather than truth.
This ugliness is not unique to our day. Looking back in history, it is
easy to understand the distress Molière must have felt when some of his
"brothers" in the church plotted to have him burnt for *blasphemy* because he wrote a play, *Le Tartuffe*. Ironically, the play itself was in-

tended as a corrective satire to help reform the institution of the church. In another instance of religiosity perverting art, when Botticelli came under the spiritual influence of the fiery priest, Savonarola, he, at the fevered priest's bidding, burnt some of his earlier "nonreligious," "sinful" artwork! He then painted a gloomy series of second-rate religious paintings. Bad art but right-minded theology. Savonarola was gratified; the human race became a little poorer.

Yet, in spite of the tragic examples of intolerance of the arts by some Christians past and present, the glory of the historical church, both Byzantine and Western, that *did* understand the arts stands in stark contrast to our own inward-looking time.

3

FALSE GUILT—TRUE GUILT

So full of artless jealousy is guilt,
It spills itself in fearing to be spilt.

SHAKESPEARE, *Hamlet*, Act IV, Scene 5

I n the arts, not to mention life in general, there should be no segregation of secular and religious subject matter. Reality, like God, is one. This is not an unusual idea. It is, after all, a derivative of St. Augustine's foundational concept embodied in *The City of God*. Augustine saw the cosmos as one unit divinely infused and all mankind as one brotherhood. He saw reality, spiritual and physical, as moving toward an unfolding of God's purposes. Reality was a cumulative advancement of mankind, materially and spiritually, through time, as history taught God's lessons through experience. Augustine rejoiced in the goodness of the arts and extolled their virtue as part of God's creation. To him, all of reality was part of the divine unfolding of history.

False Guilt

Christian artists who agonize over *what* they should create, from the point of view of what is allegedly Christian subject matter, are engaged in an exercise in futility—an exercise usually motivated by false guilt bred of a bad theology that has divided reality into "secular" and "Christian" and that perceives art as only a useful propaganda tool for "evangelization."

For the Christian, there is no taboo subject matter any more than there are evil or taboo colors. Though how we portray each subject is important, as is its context, *reality, as it is perceived, is the fit subject for the artist.* To tell the truth is our only artistic, moral imperative. To portray evil as good is sin. To portray evil *as* evil is to do right. To turn the whole world on its head and portray virtue as evil is sin. Often the context in which we portray a subject is as important as the subject itself. For instance, there is a vast difference between legitimate sexuality in art and pornography, just as there is a difference between sexual intercourse between married people and fornication or adultery. It is the context in which sexual relations take place that determines their morality, not sex itself. In artistic works, the context of events and the subject matter being portrayed determine the work's moral content and whether it is telling the truth. By truth I do not necessarily mean telling the truth about big or cosmic subjects much less theological ones. Truth can involve exploring color or texture in an abstract work. Integrity in materials, the weight and texture of an art work, or the resonance of music— all can ring true or false in a way that can be intelligently discussed and examined.

As an example of a movie telling the truth, in a figurative medium, in this case about sin and depravity, consider *Sid and Nancy,* a biographical film about the lives of Sid Vicious and his girlfriend, Nancy, made famous by the Sex Pistols, Sid Vicious' punk rock band. In the movie, the sorrow and decadence of Sid and Nancy's lives were not glamorized. The truth was told. The ugliness of the debased, anti-Christian philosophy they lived by was honestly portrayed as producing ugly results, as death-causing, tragic. To make a truthful movie like *Sid and Nancy* that is consistent with reality is ideally the goal for the Christian and non-Christian filmmaker alike.

Compromise

Many of us who are artists are not yet in the position of being able to write or choose our own material, any more than most auto workers in Detroit are engaged in designing the cars they make or setting corporate policy. We are often engaged in the making of movies, books, music, plays, etc., that do *not* wholly reflect our point of view and do not wholly tell the truth as we see it. However, the need to compromise is not a problem peculiar to those in the arts. We have to interact every day with a world that is far from ideal. For example, we pay taxes to a government that, at present, allows and often pays for abortions and has failed miserably to address the problems of a poverty-stricken under-

---

"There are, however, many 'Christian' guilt-mongers who place burdens on others that they themselves do not bear; their attitude is embodied in the *what's-Christian-about-that?* school of art critics."

---

class. We live, work, and educate our children within the confines of a fallen world.

There are too few people in the church who comprehend the artistic struggle and encourage Christians to succeed in the arts. There are, however, many "Christian" guilt-mongers who place burdens on others that they themselves do not bear; their attitude is embodied in the *what's-Christian-about-that?* school of art critics, who do not understand the arts or the daily reality of the artist's struggle. In my life as a movie-maker, for instance, there are many forces at work, most beyond my control in terms of choosing the subject matter of the movies I direct. Therefore any artistic progress I make is incremental. As artists we have to pay our dues, to suffer, to look for long-term results, to be successful, *before* we have the artistic freedom to choose the subjects we wish to express. Success must be *earned* from within the movie business and from within other artistic fields, and cannot be bought; there are no shortcuts. Few seem to understand this. They expect quick, dramatic results from what is necessarily a slow, very imperfect process.

There are hundreds of small battles we fight daily in our work and life—undramatic victories, small progress over a lifetime of work. As artists, we yearn for sympathetic critics with a knowledge of art and the historical perspective about art movements necessary to make an intelligent contribution to our work. Such understanding is, unfortunately, rare. Instead, we are often subjected to moralistic posturing on the part of Christians whose ignorance is only matched by their intransigence.

Most of us in the arts know we are fortunate to be working at all in our chosen field, much less being in command of that field! Since much of the Christian community has ignored the arts in our recent history, the Christian who wishes to learn about art must, by necessity, learn in the larger world, outside of the Christian ghetto—a ghetto that some Christians have created in a misbegotten attempt to find a sort of heaven on earth.

There is no heaven on earth. And those, like the millennialist puritans of the seventeenth century, who think we can create an earthly paradise are proven wrong in their assumptions, nor is there a place remote enough to run and hide from the world. We are called to be "in the world but not of it." We must at times create movies, television shows, books, art, music, theatre, and dance that does not mirror our worldview, while working to not be tainted in our inner being by the unbelief around us. We must not lie to ourselves about what we are doing but compromise bravely, keeping our eyes on our eventual goals. We must admit we need to walk before we can run. There will be shabby compromises aplenty necessitated by our work, not because we are artists, but because we live in a fallen world. Perhaps unfairly, artistic compromises are more misunderstood than the compromises routinely made by businessmen, teachers, lawyers, nurses, pastors, and people in professions more familiar to middle America and the church.

If an actor who was a well-known evangelical Christian played the role of a homosexual in a movie, he could expect ritual condemnation for having "sold out" or worse. Yet it is no more reasonable to believe that an actor or director or dancer is expressing approval of homosexual behavior by working with a homosexual or portraying one in a film or play, than it is to accuse an insurance salesman of "underwriting sin" because some homosexual's lover is named as the beneficiary of a life insurance policy. Nor is the merit of an artistic statement's truth less if we discover that sinners were involved in its making. The star of *Chariots of Fire*, who played Christian athlete Eric Liddel, died of AIDS. Yet does his alleged homosexual behavior lessen the virtue of that movie? I think not.

The fates of the sinful and the saved are inextricably interwoven in our fallen world. The "wheat and the tares" will be sorted out on Judgment Day, but as Christ taught us, to attempt to do the sorting now is often an exercise in futility. Because the arts and media are so visible and yet so misunderstood, Christian artists are singled out for unjustified criticism from which other professions are less apt to suffer. This in no way abrogates a Christian's individual responsibility to live morally or to speak up against immorality. But in the case of the arts and other

---

"[Artists] are often subjected to moralistic posturing on the part of Christians whose ignorance is only matched by their intransigence."

---

professions, it is foolish to expect people to be able to sort out every implied consequence, real or imagined, of how they must earn their living.

Steven Hawley

Even contemporary Christians in the arts who *have* achieved the success and skill necessary to choose their subjects and portray them exceedingly well have often been rejected by many people in the church. Thus, some excellent work that *does* reflect a Christian artist's worldview has been rejected by modern fundamentalist Christians. The brilliant novels of Walker Percy are a case in point, and there are many other examples. When the first edition of the serious Christian journal on the arts, *Image,* was printed in 1989, it had on the cover a reproduction of a painting by Steven Hawley, one of America's premier, post-modern, neo-realist painters and a believing Christian. The painting of a pear, a skeleton, and a fish has a small, painted photograph in the background of Hawley's pregnant and nude wife. *Image* received a number of vitriolic letters from outraged Christians furious over this nudity in a Christian publication. "In view of the nudity in your publication . . . take me off your mailing list." "Shocked," "horrified," and "dismayed" were typical of some of the sentiments expressed.

Yet the painting, which is now in a famous private collection, has (for any with eyes to see) a strong *biblical symbolism*. For example, novelist Harold Fickett wrote in *Image* about Hawley's painting, *Black Glass Still Life with Pear, Fish and Skeleton:*

> The painting . . . asserts its character as an altar piece. . . . the symbolism is blatant. . . . The coordination of the iconography here presents a devastating interpretation of sacrifice that re-explains to us what an altar means. . . . The three central images . . . picture three separate stages in life. We see a pregnant [nude] woman in the Polaroid on the right nearing the end of her term, the baby almost the more present for being concealed in her flesh. On the left we see a young boy—Steve's second son, Vincent—standing in one corner of the studio, with a full-sized cross set up behind him. Beside the cross there is a ladder. In the middle of these two images we have a Polaroid of a man screaming out in agony. The triptych form directs our reading of these images. Because of their reference to the crucifixion we are going to be looking at life as it leads to death. Then, too, there are interior elements that tie the three together. The little boy continues the theme of growth and development enunciated in the pregnancy. The ladder leads us to connect the boy with the man in agony, for it suggests that the boy's ascent in life as he grows will simultaneously lead to the universal crucifixion of mortality. . . . The body of the fish lies on red and white tiles. The fish, since the beginning of the church, has symbolized the Christian faith, particularly in its sacramental aspects. Christ, as the fisher of men, calls us to the altar, where he breaks the loaves and fishes, supplying a meal that satisfies our eternal hunger. . . . The life that Christ extends to us, the painter seems to be saying, He gives to creatures who in their mere flesh are nothing but bones that cannot live. (*Image* [Spring 1989])

Art historian and critic Charles Jenks, in his book *Post-Modernism*, says of Hawley's work that it "achieves the richest luminosity of surface and texture . . . [and] shows the virtuosic effects . . . Photo Realism can achieve" (New York: Rizzoli, 1987, 146–47).

To perceive the truth in Hawley's work, the angry, middle-class evangelical and fundamentalist Christians canceling subscriptions would need an artistic mental vocabulary and knowledge of art history similar to Harold Fickett. Their outrage, a manifestation of gross ignorance in the face of transcendent beauty, highlights the uphill battle any talented

Christian artist will endure in expecting any understanding or encouragement from some of his fellow Christians.

Cross-Purposes

As an illustration of the gulf separating pietistic fundamentalist Christianity and the arts, I remember an incident that took place some years ago and, at the time, left me speechless.

My book *Addicted to Mediocrity* had just been published. The cover featured a detail from Michelangelo's Sistine Chapel ceiling portraying God creating Adam. A painter with a roller brush is covering the famous fresco of the partially nude figures. He has a Christian fish symbol stitched onto his back pocket. The message is clear: some Christians are so insensitive to the arts that they are metaphorically painting out art altogether.

A few days after the book came out, I was speaking at an evangelical gathering where a famous fundamentalist preacher was in attendance. He and his wife were leaders of a number of organizations that claimed to be "bringing God back into American life." This pastor congratulated me on the book. He said he had not read it yet but liked the cover, which, as he put it, expressed just what he had been saying about art. "It was about time," he said, "that someone said what needed saying about *getting rid of nudity in art!*" It slowly dawned on me that this man *assumed* that the cover of the book was *advocating* the exact attitude it was satirizing!

Oddly enough, a similar incident occurred in regard to another book I co-authored. A friend in the movie business had read *A Modest Proposal,* a Swiftian satire examining the anti-life ideas embodied by the abortion industry and new eugenics movement. In one passage, we "advocated" using fetuses as a source of protein. This woman congratulated me on having the nerve to *propose* what she thought was a perfectly logical idea! My views were so far out of line with hers that what to me was a far-fetched, obviously satirical, even sick suggestion seemed to her a serious, logical proposal!

These two gross misunderstandings symbolize how very out-of-step Christians in the arts are with both fundamentalist Christianity *and* fundamentalist secularism.

In addition to being misunderstood, the Christian artist must contend with two other problems: first, the Christian community's reaction to the highly secularized media, and second, the effects of post-Victorian middle-class values on society—effects that have replaced the tough, raw, real, robust absolutes of Scripture with something akin to the saccharine anti-reality embodied in the "family entertainment" of the Disney movies.

The artist's response to the first problem, fear of aggressive secularism by fellow Christians, should be love and understanding. Christians and Christian ideas have taken an ideological beating in this century—a beating often administered by a hostile media. However, in the case of the second point, offended false pietistic sensibilities, the artist cannot tell lies for the sake of appeasing some Christians who have absorbed (by cultural osmosis) dainty, middle-class values. The world *is* a rough, violent, gritty, and fleshy place of immense joy *and* sorrow. That some people are offended by reflections of reality, even beautiful pro-life reflections as in Hawley's painting of his nude pregnant wife, is not the fault of the artist. And it is not the artist who should change what he or she is expressing to accommodate such wrong-headed ideas. To do so would be to use his or her God-given talents to tell lies—perhaps nice, middle-class lies, but lies nevertheless.

Reality

Art is about truth. Art is not an expression of wishful thinking. Art is about beauty, inasmuch as beauty, too, is part of truth. But there are different kinds of beauty. There is beauty in the *way* something is done as well in the actual subject matter. For instance, one can have a beautiful painting of an ugly incident—for instance, an icon showing the crude crucifixion of our Lord. Conversely, one can have a silly, sentimental photograph or painting of a beautiful subject, the kind of obscenity that typifies Playboy's soft-core porn; the decorative art of the "hotel-motel" variety that one sees displayed on countless sidewalks in tourist resorts; and the sort of "art" that some pastors now delight in hanging in their "counseling" rooms instead of the glorious icons of the historic church.

Artistic questions are more complex than a list of "dos" and "don'ts." Artists will make mistakes. Most artwork is not fully resolved; it is only a way station on the path of learning which leads to more finished, more complete work. The artist is involved in a lifetime struggle to produce anything finished, complete, and valid in his or her art. And it is the lifetime work of the artist that should, in fairness, be judged, not his or her every halting step. Artists need time, a *lifetime,* to develop their skills and to perfect their work. Beyond the individual art-

---

"The artist cannot tell lies for the sake of appeasing some Christians who have absorbed (by cultural osmosis) dainty, middle-class values."

---

ist, art movements in history need many lifetimes, each building on the last to create any permanent cultural impact.

I have for years been nonplussed by the overserious ideological, "theological" response to my own artistic endeavors by some other Christians. I have felt that people have mistaken my own efforts, such as they are—first in painting, then film—for sermons, when in fact they were often only experimental works containing many flaws. I have learned from and progressed beyond these flaws only to discover that even more remains to be learned! By the manner in which some Christians have discussed, and even savaged, my work, I assume they thought that I was trying to "say" something in the same way as, for instance, I am "saying" something in this non-fiction book. However, a non-fiction book *on* the arts is a very different thing from art itself. Color, texture, poetic nuance, and mood cannot and should not be reduced to theological categories as if art work were no more than another means of carrying on a seminarial debate.

I have had people ask me what a certain scene in a "secular" movie I directed "meant." I have felt like replying that it was not in the original script but was invented to replace some other scene we were not able to shoot due to bad weather. All that it meant was that it had rained that day. More often than not such an apparently flippant explanation would be closer to the truth than a more considered, philosophical reply when it comes to the reality of making movies.

When the first ill-fated feature I directed opened in eighty theaters in the Los Angeles area in 1986, one evangelical radio talk show took questions for three whole days from irate or supportive Christian listeners who related their "theological" reactions to the movie that "Francis Schaeffer's son had made." *The Los Angeles Times,* noting this unusual manifestation of interest in, and criticism of, a movie by the normally complacent, evangelical fundamentalist Christians, ran a piece headlined "Flock Flails Flick." The sad truth was that *Wired to Kill,* a first and flawed directing effort, did not deserve any of this attention. Had evangelical fundamentalist filmgoers noted that as a first-time feature director I had much to learn, they would have been on the right track. As it was, my movie was criticized as if it were a failed "message" movie, when in fact it was just another ultra-low budget, action, sci-fi, "horror" film directed by a first-time feature director—a half-baked footnote in cinema history, at best, soon to be relegated to late night cable TV hell! In the midst of this tempest in a very small teapot, I received a great deal of personal condemnation because the "message" of my movie was not only not "Christian," but R-rated and violent. How could *this* be a "Christian" statement? Who could "get saved" watching this? This movie wasn't like a Billy Graham movie. It wasn't inspiring like *Chariots of Fire.* Why not? Had I "sold out"? Was I still a "Christian"? In this debate, I heard few encouraging voices. Only one or two people seemed to understand that a low-budget, genre movie made for the action-horror market cannot very well be held up for comparison with a ministry-generated, gospel movie or with larger budget films such as *Chariots of Fire,* made by men like David Putnam, a producer at the pinnacle of a long and exceptional career with abundant resources and experience.

Yet I was fortunate. I knew that there was a rational, compassionate Christian alternative to the witch-hunting mentality I was encountering. I had experienced this tolerant alternative in my own home from my parents and from a number of believing Christian friends who understood something of the necessities of trying to launch a movie-making career. I had had the privilege of having a father who knew, loved, and understood film, and with whom I had shared many movie ideas before he died in 1984, including early script ideas for *Wired to Kill,* which he had liked for what it was. We had had, over the years, many a long and encouraging talk about my dream of making movies.

Thus, I had enjoyed my share of encouragement. I was not completely at the mercy of the pious mob or professionally jealous, back-biting Christian "colleagues." Had I thought that the furious criticism I was facing represented the teachings of Scripture or of the wisdom of the historic, apostolic church on the arts, and had I never known of another way of looking at culture and art other than through a nervous, middle-class, propagandistic, fundamentalist set of spectacles, then I would have been in the desperate position of trying to choose between my faith and my movie-making.

Fortunately, this was not the case; I had the privilege of enjoying a wider perspective. Not everyone employed in the arts has been so fortunate. I have observed many creative people browbeaten and finally cowed and crushed into submission. They litter the path of the evangelical fundamentalist juggernaut, chewed up, then regurgitated, by the faithful. The absence of Christians in the movie business, indeed in the arts in general, bears mute testimony to the "success" of the evangelical world in eliminating talent from its midst.

True Guilt

Just because many burdens of false guilt have been placed on Christian artists does not excuse us from heeding our consciences when pricked by the Holy Spirit. Adultery, divorce, abortion, fornication, lust for power and money, homosexual behavior, arrogance, and the other *real* temptations and sins which may beset us must be resisted with moral fortitude. These sins, which devour so many in our culture, including many Christian "leaders," produce death. In some instances, churches, in imitating the surrounding society, have begun to subtly surrender to these evils and even condone them. In these matters of spiritual and physical life and death, the Christian artist must, for the sake of his or her own soul, stand firm.

If we are to live as Christians obedient to Christ and the holy tradition of His historic church, we must, like Tolstoy, long for righteousness. And, unlike Tolstoy, who seems even in his declining years to have followed his sexual appetite more than his conscience, succeed in doing more than just wishing for sanctity! We must be sexually chaste, faithful to our spouses, good husbands and wives, good parents. We must renounce greed, divorce, and blind ambition. To even attempt to live by these normal, ageless virtues of Christian teaching sets us apart from many nonbelievers and also from an increasingly compromised church that minimizes sin in the name of "love." In today's climate of religious experience for experience sake, it is easy to forget that to love Christ is to obey Him. This love is not a feeling, experience, or a mere idea. Our love for Christ can be measured against our success in obeying His clear commands, His teaching, and in immitating His life.

Daniel

Pursuing righteousness will give us a measure of spiritual clarity of vision, the sort of wisdom Daniel possessed while in the court of Nebuchadnezzar. He participated in the court life of Babylon, yet he was not corrupted. Daniel kept himself holy, not by forming a religious ghetto or school separated from Babylonian culture, but while being a part of the pagan governmental system without being consumed by it.

Daniel was able to speak for God because he was *in* the court, not outside of it, because he worked *within* the sinful structure of the regime. He was deemed "ten times better" at what he did academically than his non-Jewish competition. He was measured by the academic standards of his day and not found wanting. He was in the right place at the right time. Babylon was no worse a challenge to personal morality than Hollywood. Daniel stood; we can too.

The Roman Soldier

In the New Testament, there is a similar example of someone called to remain in the world without surrendering to it. John the Baptist, in Luke 3:14, exhorts a soldier to moral conduct while remaining in the immoral Roman army. He told him to not extort money, not to accuse people falsely, and to be content with his pay. John the Baptist told him to be, in effect, in the world—in this case the Roman army—but not of it. That John the Baptist advised the Roman soldier to *remain* in the military may be surprising from our point of view. The Roman army served dictatorial, imperial Rome and was a violent, profane, pagan organization. Yet John did *not* order the soldier to leave the military and be a missionary instead. John told him to be a moral person in the midst of immorality.

It is a hard task to direct our lives and minds away from the false burdens of spiritual guilt that call us to be out of the world and out of life and toward the true call of God to be in the world but not of it. It is an undertaking complicated by the fact that to be a good artist and a

---

"In today's climate of religious experience for experience sake, it is easy to forget that to love Christ is to obey Him."

---

faithful Christian is, by definition, to offend the pietists who control the thought of many churches today.

Christ deeply offended the Pharisees, and if we are to live as good artists and good Christians, we will offend their modern descendants as well. But Christ also stood up to Satan and was loving to the "least of these." Unlike the simplistic rules of fundamentalism, the true Christian life is a balancing high-wire act. We will fall from time to time, but there is a net. Its name is repentance, confession, penance, and forgiveness.

We can be sure that the Roman soldier had many problems trying to follow John's instructions while also serving Caesar. But John, like Christ and unlike today's pietistic Christian leadership, was never in the facile business of making things easy for his followers.

Issues

The artist must struggle through many issues. One is the question of performing other peoples' works of art. Most art is performance art or its equivalent. A concert violinist, an actor, a movie director, a book or magazine editor—all have a job to do. It is a way of honorably earning a living; it is a way of obeying the biblical command to use our talents.

If Christ is truly Lord of all life, then an artist who is part of an orchestra performing a symphony by Mahler is praising God just as much as a member of a church choir singing an excerpt from the *Messiah*. An actor with a part in a second-rate movie he does not even like is praising God by using his talent just as much as a missionary feeding the hungry in some flea-ridden hellhole.

What we make when we can freely choose our subject is important, but the *how* and the *why* are equally important. Our creative work may be on projects that will not reflect what we believe to be true. But the artist needs to learn, to work, to succeed enough to be given the opportunity to call his or her own shots. Like Daniel, who surely found Babylon less than ideal yet used his opportunity when given it, we must slog forward one step at a time and attempt to be good at what we do—"ten times better"—to succeed and be like Daniel, in the right place at the right time, to be moral people in the midst of immorality.

Bad Advice from Worse People

We as Christians need the help, guidance, and advice of other believers. But we must be careful, as artists, to have realistic expectations about this human advice. Just because someone is a believing, practicing Christian does not mean he or she will have the wisdom, knowledge, or sympathy to advise us knowledgeably about our artistic work. Just because someone *claims* that God has "laid something on his heart" does not mean God has! The teacher, friend, or family member may or may not know enough about a particular field of endeavor to give good advice.

We must be wise in choosing those from whom we seek personal and professional advice and to whom we present our fragile ideas. In their infancy, ideas can be aborted if handled by the insensitive hands of well-meaning but ignorant believers or nonbelievers.

As Christians in the arts, we should pray that God would give us one or two understanding colleagues to know as friends. Since all people are created in God's image, whether they acknowledge Him or not, there are many sensible and wise nonbelievers to whom one may look for good artistic, aesthetic, and career advice.

In my own experience as a moviemaker, some of my greatest discouragements have come from contact with some other Christians and their vitriolic criticism. However, to be candid, there are many areas about which I am ignorant and judgmental myself. I have often been less than kind in my own public critique of some fellow Christians. To receive harsh treatment at the hands of my fellow believers is, in my

---

"Just because someone *claims* that God has 'laid something on his heart' does not mean God has!"

---

case, really no more than to get a dose of my own caustic medicine. However, my own comeuppance aside, it is a tragedy that so many Christians who seek to work in the arts and media receive so little *knowledgeable* encouragement.

Without wishing to judge individual motives, there seems to be an uglier undercurrent to some of the criticism given to those who, like me, attempt to work in the "secular" world. As the old saw goes, misery loves company. And those who by choice or fate work in the evangelical ghetto and have settled for its small, creatively unsatisfying boundaries are sometimes resentful of people who attempt to escape, let alone who enjoy some small measure of "secular" success.

4

ART VERSUS MESSAGE: WHAT IS ART?

art. (art), n. 1. The production or expression of what is beauti-
ful, appealing, or of more than ordinary significance. 2. An
illustration. 3. A department of skilled performance. 4. (pl.)
Liberal arts. 5. Skilled workmanship. 6. Cunning.
7. Artificiality in behavior. 8. An artifice.

I s art propaganda? Is it entertainment? What *is* art? To understand a
work of art, one needs knowledge of the technique employed, the
artist, or at least its historical context. Art, contrary to today's ideas of
"enlightened" egalitarianism, is rarely for the masses, though there have
been periods in history when the general public has been unusually well
informed—for example, Orthodox Christian Byzantine Constantinople,
the High Middle Ages, and the Florentine Renaissance, or Elizabethan
England, when theater was appreciated by the general public much as
film is today. At one time the working class represented by the
craftsmen's guilds supported some of the greatest artistic achievements
in the Florentine Renaissance. For instance, the armorers' guild commissioned Donatello in 1416 to sculpt his famous St. George.

As an example of the common people's awareness of the great artistic achievements of the Florentine Renaissance and their appreciation of
the arts, take this quote of Benedetto Dei, a Florentine merchant who
wrote to a friend in Venice in 1472: "Go through all the cities of the
world and nowhere will you ever be able to find artists . . . equal to
those we now have in Florence" (*Art of the Western World* [New York:
Summit Books, 1989], 90).

In Holland, during the "golden age" of painting in the seventeenth century, the common people, in contrast to the nobility, supported the work of the painters who proliferated in that era. Peter Jansz, Jan Vermeer, Pieter De Hooch, Jan Steen, Willem Kalf, Jacob Van Ruisdael, Frans Hals, and Rembrandt were only some of the many painters that produced the portraits, landscapes, and still lifes that were purchased by Holland's merchants, craftsmen, and laborers. Some of the greatest pieces of art produced in that period were purchased by blacksmiths, cobblers, tailors, and bakers. Their interest in a pictorial examination of everyday life led them to support the greatest artists of northern Europe.

However, art is rarely casual. Art is a form of human expression pursued professionally and vocationally full-time for life. Michelangelo is said to have joked about his cradle-to-grave dedication to his art: "With my wet-nurse's milk, I sucked in the hammer and chisel I use for my statues."

All of an artist's works are not of equal value. Artists reach an artistic peak, recognized later in time. His or her progress—like all human history—is linear, from less experience to more experience and accomplishment. The artist, at some point, achieves maximum productivity combined with maximum skill, and this height of effort intersects the highest level of his or her technical experience, producing at that time the artist's masterpieces—the millennial golden age of one life, if you will.

All human expression has intrinsic value, but not all is equal. Art is the highest form of human expression when the artist expresses truth about his or her chosen subject through accomplished, professional ability, natural talent, hard work, and discipline. Through history, art styles have changed, but the basic nature of the vocational, lifelong effort of the artist remains the constant, necessary ingredient for producing great art. Hard work and lonely pilgrimage have been the common lot of artists throughout history. Rejection by other people remains the basic fact of life to many artists.

What Is Art?

Art is different from craft. The crafts tend to serve some literal function, for instance, as furniture or pottery. Art is *pure* expression in the sense that art is not useful or practical in the same way as crafts might be.

People make art because we, as humans, respond to the deep calling of our creative, heavenly Father. The capacity to produce and enjoy art is one of the abilities that makes humans uniquely different from other creatures. Art is the expression of the divine *uselessness* of beauty, truth, and reality.

To help understand what art is, let us look at another area of divinely inspired expression: prayer. Sometimes we pray because we want some specific things: a home, a wife, money, political change, whatever. This is the spiritual equivalent to the physical craft—useful

---

"The existence of the arts mirrors God's own extravagant creativity, His creation of "useless" beauty, His abundant expression of variety, and His attention to aesthetic detail."

---

and for a specific purpose. Sometimes, however, we pray to worship, to express our love for God, to express a nameless sense of fullness in our spirit, sorrow, or anxiety beyond words. This is equivalent to what art is in relationship to craft.

Art is useless but far from meaningless. Our capacity to be sustained by useless beauty, meaning, and truth—for instance, the comfort of home and hearth—is one of the reasons why we can be certain that we are created creatures of infinite value. Theories of the evolution of the species may explain biological complexities and changes; however, they stand mute in offering an explanation of Beethoven's Ninth Symphony or why we love it.

Our enjoyment of crafts can always be explained by ulterior motives; for example, the need to use them in some way to better our daily lives. However, our enjoyment of the useless beauty of art and worship can only be explained by the fact that we are responding to a larger call than the mere needs of survival. Man does *not* live by bread alone. The arts are for sustaining human life just as much as food, worship, water, air, and love.

The existence of the arts mirrors God's own extravagant creativity, His creation of "useless" beauty, His abundant expression of variety, and His attention to aesthetic detail. God has a commitment to beauty—beauty which is real and not merely in the eye of the beholder, beauty that exists in a quantifiable, abstract sense.

I believe that beauty exists independent of the personal taste of the observer. In this sense aesthetics are as absolute as physics. This does not mean that we, in our fallen state, can ever achieve an absolute understanding of what is beautiful. However, we can perceive abstract beauty as the divine signature on nature. In this fallen world our sense of beauty is also fallen; therefore, tastes vary and people will disagree over what constitutes beauty. However, God will show us what is beautiful and what is not by creative example in the new heaven and the new earth. Created nature already points the aesthetic way. God said His creation was "good." This was an absolute statement covering all aspects of reality, including aesthetics and worship.

Even in the fallen world, nature and the highly developed, God-given skills in the arts help us define *aesthetics*. There is a reason why sensitive and tasteful people react negatively to synthetic, highly processed materials.

When art is deliberately corrupted to become "useful," it is as repugnant as it would be to ban sacramental worship from the Christian life to be replaced only with "utilitarian" social work. There is a place for practical charity, but also, as the sinful woman who perfumed Christ's hair and washed His feet with her tears understood, a place for repentance and worship, for its own sake, for the love of God Himself. Much of our lives is spent pursuing tangible, measurable goals, but life soon becomes gray and pointless if our souls cannot explore beyond the pragmatic. In this sense all art is abstract. All art is a language of the spirit, even if words, as in theater, are its medium.

Art is all at once one of the most pointless of human luxuries and one of the basic necessities of life. All cultures, even those that are materially poverty stricken, produce art. This should tell us something concerning the nature of people and their need to express themselves. The appreciation and creation of art is a manifestation of the love of God for people, manifested by His willingness to share that most rare of all gifts with His mere creatures: creativity.

Propaganda v. Art

To use art as propaganda, even for good causes, is a waste. This is not to say that art does not at times legitimately express a particular viewpoint; because art is human expression, it will often express an opinion. But in genuine art, the expression of a particular, political, or human viewpoint is unselfconscious and is submerged in favor of expressing truths, common to the experiences of all people. A particular viewpoint may emerge along with many other elements that make up the integrated totality of the artwork in question.

The expression of political, cultural, or sociological viewpoints, should not be the motivating force behind the artist's work. Art soon

---

"To use art as propaganda, even for good causes, is a waste."

---

slides toward propaganda if the motivation for it is too utilitarian and immediate. It ceases to be art and is less honest than forthright proselytizing. Picasso's painting protesting the brutality of the destruction of Guernica by the Nazi's bombs is a good political poster but, I suspect, not his best artwork. Oliver Stone's leftist political propaganda statements in movie form, will be forgotten as soon as the political climate changes, thus rendering them unintelligible and obsolete. When his movies are forgotten, a film like *Moonstruck* will always have an audience. That is because the narcissistic politics of the post-Vietnam generation will someday be unintelligible, but the human race will always understand a love story.

The existence of art is a manifestation of *who* people are, a witness to the character of God in people. Art is not to be prostituted, even for good causes. Art is not to be tampered with for a message's sake or for expediency's sake, any more than mother love should be manipulated as a tool of the state, to serve something "better," "higher." It *is* already the better thing in itself. Watching a mother breast-feeding her baby does not teach us about love; it *is* love in action. The purpose of art is not to teach us about God; it *is* God's love for us in action. Jesus did not only come to earth to teach us about goodness, He *is* goodness. Art is not a means to an end; it *is* an end in itself, a reflection of the name of God, *I Am.* Therefore, the idea of producing "Christian" art, music, novels, plays, etc., as it is commonly understood by many earnest but misguided fundamentalists and evangelicals, is wrong.

Dr. Hans Rookmaaker addressed this point when he wrote in his book *Modern Art and the Death of a Culture* ([Downers Grove, IL: Inter-Varsity, 1970], 228–230):

> In a way there is no specifically Christian art. One can distinguish only good and bad art, art which is sound and good from art which is false. . . . A work of art is not good when we know that the artist was a Christian: it is good when we perceive it to be good. Nor is a work bad if we know that the artist was a hater of God. It would be possible to make an exhibition of beautiful Picassos. The exhibition would possibly not do justice to the spirit that drove Picasso on in his creativity, yet it would show us that the man is human. . . . Art needs no justification. The mistake of many art theorists, (and not only of Christian ones), is to try to give art a meaning or a sense by showing that it "does something." . . . Art needs no such excuse. It has its own meaning.

Craft v. Propaganda v. Art

Naturally the divisions between art and craft consist of many shades of gray. Classical Greek vases, Gothic cathedrals, the jewel-like modernist architectural creations of I. M. Pei come to mind as functional creations defying easy categories. For instance, Pei's buildings and Gothic cathedrals serve a function, are "useful," but the creative genius of their makers transcends the merely functional. The Dallas Symphony Center, The Bank of China in Hong Kong, the breathtakingly beautiful National Gallery extension in Washington, D.C., with its razor-thin angles in stone, and Pei's other buildings have the weight and permanence of masterpieces on a par with Michelangelo's architectural artwork, for instance, the Medici library in Florence. The mastery of architectural geometry and light in Pei's work surely transcends the division between what is art and what is architectural craft. Genius confounds simple definitions. The creators of Chartres Cathedral or Santa Sophia in Constantinople, cannot be labeled mere artisans. In fact, Byzantine and Gothic architecture is an expression of that uniquely Christian mind-set found in the Europe of St. Thomas Aquinas and St. Francis and the Byzantine empire of Justinian I. Gothic architecture was a heroic departure from the Romanesque past. In a way, it was the real new beginning or "renaissance" in European art looking forward not backward. The Renaissance was less radical of a new beginning than was the explosion of Gothic creativity.

G. K. Chesterton captures its advent well. In his 1933 book *Saint Thomas Aquinas*, ([New York: Doubleday, 1956] 41, 91), we read:

> Nobody can understand the greatness of the thirteenth century, who does not realise that it was a great growth of new things produced by a living thing. In that sense it was really bolder and freer than what we call the Renaissance, which was a resurrection of old things discovered in a dead thing. [Pagan Roman culture] in that sense medievalism was not a Renascence, but rather a Nascence. It did not model its temples upon the tombs, or call up dead gods from Hades. It made an architecture as new as modern engineering: indeed it still remains the most modern architecture. . . . gleaming into the northern skies, partly picked out with gold and bright colours; a new flight of architecture, as startling as flying-ships.

Some craft becomes art. Some art becomes propaganda. Some art entertains without becoming mere entertainment. These lines are real but not fixed. Yet, special exceptions aside, there is a definite difference between craft and art. Craft is immensely worthwhile and often adds as much beauty to our lives as does artwork. To distinguish art from craft is not an attempt either to aggrandize art or belittle craft, but simply to recognize each for what it is.

Eternal Meanings in Art

As the fathers of the West from St. Constantine to Martin Luther understood, reality comes from God. All reality, therefore, even fallen reality, is worth exploring. Art, like science, explores this fallen reality and also creates new realities. Art continues God's creative process and even enlarges on it. By recombining materials God created and using His creative gift to make unique works of art, people create objects and ideas that exist as distinct entities apart from the artist and God.

God endowed us with the capacity to make moral choices. Remarkably, He also has given us the ability, through art, to create *beyond* His own creation, to make our own worlds and universes, for good or ill. Yet within His will, we fulfill our creative destinies by exercising our God-given free will.

All art serves God's purposes by its very existence. As Leonardo da Vinci wrote of the artistic mind, it is "a copy of the divine mind, since it operates freely." By responding to art, we make choices, expressed by our reactions. In this way there is a dialogue between the artist and the audience, a dialogue that bridges the centuries and binds all humanity together in a common experience. We can know Leonardo da Vinci or the artists who created Ravenna's Byzantine mosaics, as well as our neighbor across the street—perhaps better.

From the pre-historic scratchings on a cave wall in southern France to the ceiling of the Sistine Chapel or the Byzantine art works of St. Marco in Venice, art speaks with one voice: Mankind is special; mankind is transcendent in his spirit; mankind's existence has eternal meaning. Art communicates in universal terms from one generation to the next.

Observing and enjoying art gives deeper meaning to our love of God and God's creation, humanity. Art thus leads us toward God. This is why in historic Christian worship icons are not casually used but are mandatory. If Christ has redeemed all things and come in the flesh, then art, too, can be used in worship and praise.

Art can be full of comedy, wit, and humor, and be a dazzling experience that wakens the spirit. Art is the stone against which we sharpen our wit and intellect, and also our emotions and senses. Sexuality, humor, fear, worship, sense of weight and texture, love, enjoyment of beauty, and terror are only some of the emotions and senses that art stimulates. Our senses were created by a God who gave us bodies, minds, and souls; our senses need not be at war with our spirits but are one with them when we submit to the lordship of Christ. Thus, to enjoy art, we need not abandon our intellect and merely *feel*. Art communicates in concrete terms, expressing ideas, ways of seeing, and content as well as human emotion. Contrary to popular, modern critical scholarship, we *can* look at art and know the intent of the artist or author. As fellow human beings, we have more in common with them than distinctives that keep us apart. Gender and race and cultural experience pale in contrast to the common human bond between all of God's children.

Great art is often explosive; it defines and gives meaning to whole peoples, periods of history, and nations. It has the capacity to show us what is important in life and to define our perceptions of reality. It shows us ourselves. "Art," said Henry James, "is nothing more than the shadow of humanity."

"Observing and enjoying art gives deeper meaning to our love of God and God's creation, humanity. Art thus leads us toward God. This is why in historic Christian worship icons are not casually used but are manditory."

The gentle events of daily life portrayed in Vermeer's paintings infuse the ordinary with dignity. For instance, in one work, *Young Women With a Water Jug* (1665), we see a mother at home, at peace with God and her neighbor. By painting her, the artist has made her life an event, part of the fabric of the important things in life worth celebrating. The translucent beauty of Botticelli's *Primavera* reinforces the Orthodox Christian idea that nature is good in itself, that our world is a world informed by rare, symbolic, divine beauty, and that the graces are just as important as commerce to man's existence. It also shows us a sexuality in which base lust is absent. Botticelli's work speaks in universal human terms, as relevant today as the day he finished it.

Great art, while challenging our ideas, nevertheless often restrains man's rapacity and sinful tendency toward chaos and destruction; it assists in creating societies that know their worth. In that sense, the art of Shakespeare *is* Elizabethan England. The art of the Renaissance *is* Florence. The art of Byzantium is Constantinople and Orthodox Christianity.

And, conversely, the "art" of the subway graffiti artists in New York *is* New York today.

It is no accident that tyrants have hesitated to destroy artistically rich cities like Florence and Paris. Or at least, as in the case of Hitler, the tyrant's minions have disobeyed destructive orders, thus saving those cities for posterity. And it is no coincidence that the sack of the artistically rich city of Constantinople, in 1204, by the barbarous Latin "Christians" of Northern Europe has been called "the greatest tragedy of history." The drastic measures taken by some Protestants during the social upheavals following the Reformation, the smashing of statuary and other artwork in Roman Catholic churches, has rightly earned condemnation by civilized people.

The existence of the arts is the most tangible evidence of the existence of the soul. When a person stands quietly looking at a painting, he is bearing witness, consciously or unconsciously, to the vast difference between people and the rest of nature. The arts create a climate in which ideas concerning mankind's destiny can be understood.

Freedom for Art

When artists are given freedom of expression, they contribute to a climate of intellectual and political freedom for the whole culture. It is no coincidence that the ugliest, grayest, and dullest parts of the world today are places where people have been persecuted for their ideas. The listless grime that was the Communist bloc owes some of its haplessness to its imprisonment of the arts. Communism has censored and coerced art until it has become mere propaganda. The visual ugliness of Communist society, or societies recently dominated by Communists, is a result of communism's ideological misunderstanding of the human soul.

It is not by chance that the independent, relatively free republics of Tuscan, Italy, which came into being in the twelfth and thirteenth centuries, produced the climate of tolerance which in turn led to the creative explosion that was the Renaissance. Freedom, as it nourishes people's souls, produces creative results. Nor is it coincidental that in Christian Constantinople the arts flourished as trade was encouraged and religious tolerance of Jews and others was practiced.

The lowest common denominator is *not* the right standard to set in the arts or any other field of endeavor. As the black conservative American economists Thomas Sowell and Glenn C. Loury have so amply demonstrated in their writings, a purely egalitarian view of life produces dreadful results because it is not a reflection of the reality of human existence but merely a wishful, utopian idea. There is nothing wrong with high and even exclusive standards of complexity in the arts. There

---

"The existence of the arts is the most tangible evidence of the existence of the soul. . . . The arts create a climate in which ideas concerning mankind's destiny can be understood."

---

is nothing wrong with the high degree of sophistication needed to make a great work of art, or the study or knowledge necessary to appreciate it. In our society, all people may have equality under the law, but it is absurd to pretend that all people are equal in skills or talents. That everything is not instantly accessible to everyone is a fact of life, not a condemnation or a put-down of any particular people who are less talented or knowledgeable in some areas than others.

The arts and humanities can be enjoyed on many levels. No one need feel left out because no one is totally included. The appreciation of art, like life and spirituality, is a journey. We never reach our goal completely, but there is meaning in the effort.

Religion in Art

A great deal of art in Christian history has had religious subject matter. Sometimes this has been mere church-inspired propaganda; sometimes, as with the frescoes of Fra Angelico, the Byzantine mosaics of Ravenna, Constantinople, and Venice, it has been a genuine artistic declaration of faith and an exercise in religious contemplation by the artist—what John Brown alluded to as an "Art . . . quickened from above and from within" (*Horoe Subsecivoe: Notes on Art*).

Fra Angelico, a monk in the monastery of San Marco in Florence, was an artist to whom the expression of religious content in his frescoes was a very personal and natural declaration of his belief and interest in biblical themes. Vasari, the first biographer of the artists of the Renaissance, wrote of him: "Fra Angelico was a man of simplicity, and most holy in his ways. . . . [He] would never have taken his brushes in hand without first offering a prayer. He never painted a crucifix without tears streaming down his cheeks" (*Artists of the Renaissance* [London: Allen Lane, 1965—First published in 1568], 119).

One of Fra Angelico's principal paintings, *Descent from the Cross*, is described by Michael Wood.

> Within a pristine Tuscan landscape, Christ is lowered from the cross. As Mary Magdalene reverently kisses Christ's feet, John the Evangelist assists Nicodemus in lowering the sacred body. Cosimo's [Cosimo de' Medici was Fra Angelico's supporter and patron] namesake, Saint Cosmos, shows the crown of thorns and the nails, while a host of mourners crowds around the Virgin. . . . Hushed, respectful, and completely devout, the assembled figures present a scene that equates clarity of form, purity of color, and rationally conceived properties with transcendent spirituality. The mode of expression is dignified, rational, and human. (*Art of the Western World*, 102)

Art has often been commissioned by the church and religious institutions, the subject matter often chosen for the artist by the patron. Some artists have made the subject matter of commissions, religious or otherwise, their own, as with the intensely spiritual Michelangelo and his Sistine Chapel, thus going beyond the limits of the commission while faithfully fulfilling it.

Michelangelo's relationship to his patrons in the church is instructive and proves that even though it was fraught with difficulties, in the end it was a mutually beneficial arrangement typical of the stimulation the church often provided for the arts in his period of history. *David* was commissioned by the directors of the Duomo, Florence's cathedral. Thus it was the church that commissioned this most famous and sublime monumental nude sculpture of the human figure. The tempestuous friendship between Pope Julius II and Michelangelo resulted in the pope summoning Michelangelo to Rome to produce a variety of works—the Sistine Chapel frescoes and the figures for an unfinished, monumental tomb for Julius among them. These and other commissions were almost completely in the control of the artist. Michelangelo even forbade the pope

---

"Many a believing artist, composer, writer, and architect has found that as they acquire experience, prestige, and opportunity their works have been naturally infused by the love of God. . . . Art, prayer, and confession merge into a cry from the heart of a man to the heart of his God."

---

from setting foot inside the Sistine Chapel until he had finished the great work—a work that nearly killed him as he worked against almost insurmountable odds of heat, cold, sickness, and a dislocated neck (from bending back to paint above him for four years). He thus appropriated the commission.

Michelangelo was a deeply spiritual, Christian man. His religious works, especially late in his life, were a personal expression of faith. His many poems express a deep Christian faith and contemplation. Thus his religious works for the church were much more than mere commissions. Just before his death he wrote,

> My course of life already has attained,
> Through stormy seas, and in a flimsy vessel,
> The common port, at which we land to tell,
> All conduct's cause and warrant, good or bad.
> (*The Complete Work of Michelangelo*
> [New York: Artabras Books, 1964], 541)

Here the great artist speaks of facing judgment and of heaven: "The common port." His last work was an evocative unfinished pietà.

Many a believing artist, composer, writer, and architect has found that as they acquire experience, prestige, and opportunity their works have been naturally infused by the love of God. This has not come about out of some urge to propagandize but rather out of the artist's natural conversation through his art with his God. Then, like the first light of morning, the darkness flees, and the horizon for a moment becomes a seamless sphere touching the sky. Art, prayer, and confession merge into a cry from the heart of a man to the heart of his God.

5

THE ART KILLERS

It is a revealing symptom of our cultural malaise that for two decades our academic institutions have been shaken by spasms of radical reevaluation of what to do with [art and literature] ranging from uneasy self doubt to incipient panic to the exhilaration of an intellectual witch's sabbath.

ROBERT ALTER, *Commentary Magazine,* (March 1990)

A curse of our own time is that there has been the unwitting collusion between the unlikely bedfellows of middle America and the politicized leftist academic elite to do away with standards of excellence in the arts and humanities.

Standards of Excellence

Middle America tends to resent anything that has not sufficiently been "dumbed down" to accommodate it. The egalitarian left, for its part, is reflexively against anything that is not part of its great leveling of all society into a gray "equality." Witness the destruction of the public school system or the abandonment of standards in many academic and artistic fields as utopian dreams of "affirmative action," "equality," or "learning from other non-Western cultural traditions" have taken hold. These are pursued in spite of the resultant lowered standards of academic and artistic excellence.

The well-known black professor of political economy at Harvard's Kennedy School of Government, Glenn C. Loury, in describing one aspect of this phenomena as it has affected the black community in America, writes:

> So widespread has such practice become that, especially in the elite levels of employment, all blacks must now deal with the perception that without a quota, they would not have their jobs. All blacks, some of our "leaders" seem proud to say, owe their accomplishments to political pressures for diversity. And the effects of such thinking may be seen in our response to almost every instance of racially differential performance. When blacks cannot pass a high school proficiency test as a condition of obtaining a diploma—throw out the test. When black teachers cannot exhibit skills at the same level as whites, the very idea of testing teachers' skills is attacked. If black athletes less frequently achieve the minimal academic standards set for those participating in inter-collegiate sports, then let us promulgate for them a separate, lower standard, even as we accuse of racism those suggesting the need for a standard in the first place. ("Achieving the 'Dream,'" A paper delivered February 12, 1990 at the Heritage Foundation, Washington, D.C.)

Ideology has proven stronger than historic fact, let alone common sense. The humanities and the arts are suffering. For example, in the universities the *great books*, books that were once regarded by generations of Western scholars as being indisputably the classic foundational works of Western thought, have been abandoned as required reading.

Consider the actions of the present-day heir of the American Left, leader of the American welfare plantation, perpetual candidate and media creation, the Rev. Jesse Jackson. History will record the day he led a march at Stanford University chanting, "Ho, Ho, Western culture has got to go!" This was an effort to "reform" curriculum and to get rid of the great books, the classics, as required reading, to be replaced by less "elitist"—read, less *Western*—works. In an article in *Newsweek* (October 16, 1989), Jackson was quoted as saying, "Wherever I focus, others follow. I can bring the light." Yet one wonders what "light" Jackson and those of like mind will use to replace the light of Jewish-Christian civilization. If it is time to bid Western civilization good-bye, which models of social and artistic behavior are we now to follow? Who will be our heroes? Saddam Hussein? Idi Amin? Yassar Arafat? Stalin? Castro? The Visigoths? Who?

Allan Bloom made the following observation about the American university landscape, where those who disparage Western culture have triumphed in removing the classics from the curriculum and in destroying any sense of the permanent achievements of Western thought in human history. He writes:

> Such education is little more than propaganda, and propaganda that does not work. . . . This gradual stilling of the old political and religious echoes in the soul of the young accounts for the difference between the students I knew at the beginning of my teaching career [in the 1950s], and those I face now. The loss of the [great] books has made them narrower and flatter. Narrower because they lack what is most necessary, a real basis for discontent with the present and aware-

---

"The 'moron factor' that dominates intellectual life in middle America is not the result of an accident; it is a choice which reflects the market response. . . . Popular culture exists at this level because rubbish sells."

> ness that there are alternatives to it. . . . The very models . . . have vanished. Flatter, because without interpretation of things, without the poetry or the imagination's activity, their souls are like mirrors, not of nature, but of what is around. The refinement of the mind's eye that permits it to see the delicate distinctions among men, among their deeds and motives, and constitutes real taste, is impossible without the assistance of literature in the grand style. (*The Closing of the American Mind* [New York: Simon and Schuster, 1987], 61)

Middle America may not think it has much in common with the Rev. Jesse Jackson and those other latter Vandals who would sack Constantinople anew, burn Paris, blow up Florence, and banish the light of Western culture in favor of third-world folklore, but in its own way, God-fearing middle America also wants Western culture to go. Meat-and-potatoes middle America resents intellectual and artistic complexity—anything that takes a little thought to approach. Witness the miserable addiction to TV programming in our nation, evangelical sermons, the level of "teaching" many parents accept for their children, and the majority of "Christian" books, including certain recent best-selling "Christian novels." The "moron factor" that dominates intellectual life in middle America is not the result of an accident; it is a choice which reflects the market response to the high-calorie/low-protein taste of the public. And the market does not lie—popular culture exists at this level because rubbish sells.

Yet, while Christians have been absent from the cultural arena, others have been hard at work. Middle American Christendom may have slumbered, but a whole cavalry of deconstructionist termites have been awake and hard at their destructive labors. Typical of these labors have been those of the practitioners of feminist witchery.

Artistic Whores

Who will answer the politically radical feminists masquerading as scholars who have reduced "literary criticism" to their war against "patriarchal tyranny" hand-in-glove with "capitalism?" Who will offer an alternative, transcendent vision of literature to university students confronted by strident feminists who *seriously* debate the "literary" merits of "vaginal criticism" versus "clitoral hermeneutics"? Those confronted by the state of the arts and humanities today are likely to be inquiring into a monstrous spectacle, one in which the prevailing trends in literary artistic theory run to deconstructionism, Marxism, "third worldism," and feminism. Today, literary criticism is dominated by claims that all meanings in art are only created by the audience, that there are no universal meanings, that art and words are nothing more than the subjective playthings of the critic, that the original intent of the artist-author cannot be understood. In other words, we as humans are really all islands, unable to communicate with each other, and with no common human bonds that can transcend gender, race, religion, and politics. In other words, art is dead.

As George Steiner has recently written in his book, *Real Presence* (Chicago: University of Chicago Press, 1989), the new literary criticism ridicules the search for truth in art. It even calls into doubt the basic idea that language is able to communicate meaning from one person to another, let alone through art or literature. This form of artistic suicide pretending to the throne of literary criticism also denies the existence of God. Thus, this *deconstructionism* teaches that one can discern no eternal meaning in human communication. This once obscure French theory is now dominant on American campuses.

Steiner, a long-time fellow of Churchill College at Cambridge and a professor of literature at Geneva University in Switzerland, has concluded that ultimately it is impossible to really believe in the arts or in aesthetics, unless one believes in God and the meaning His existence

"Ironically, today's critics and academics no longer believe in the ability of art to communicate ordinary *human* meanings, but they certainly *do* believe that art can communicate *political* meanings."

gives to our lives and our attempts to communicate. He goes so far as to argue that the repudiation of God rules out all possibilities of real artistic creation. Just as there can be no criticism without a work of art to criticize, so there can be no art without Creation itself standing at the root of all creativity.

Sadly, Steiner seems to be one of the lone voices from the academic establishment even willing to question the prevailing deconstructionist, anti-art mood.

The arts are in as much of a predicament as the humanities are in the universities which Steiner discusses. Here, too, Christians are conspicuous by their absence. As we have seen, many Christians who should know better either misunderstand the arts in general, or worse, like many so-called Christian publishers and musicians, think of themselves only in regard to their evangelical, fundamentalist propaganda potential as they attempt to "reach the world through their art."

Peter Shaw, literary scholar and journalist, has written one of the best, most readable and most provocative books concerning the plight of the humanities. In *The War Against the Intellect* (Iowa City: University of Iowa Press, 1989), Shaw argues, in a series of essays, that the humanities have been brought to the edge of a new Dark Age.

It is as if the deconstructionists, the feminists, and the other modern critics in the fields of literature, art, and the humanities resent the fact that there was ever an age of moral certainty when people knew who they were, what they meant to say, and above all, in what they *believed*. To the modern critic, people of moral or artistic certainty are suspect. Because the modern relativist cannot imagine herself feeling any moral certainty, she is sure no one else can either, now or ever! Thus, modern criticism seeks to turn even pre-nineteenth-century art and literature into "modern" art, drama, and literature by investing it with the cynicism of our lost modernity. By divesting the past of its meaning, today's scholars rob future generations of their common human heritage. With the humanities and arts being guarded by friends like these in our universities, they need no enemies!

Ironically, today's critics and academics no longer believe in the ability of art to communicate ordinary *human* meanings, but they certainly *do* believe that art can communicate *political* meanings. Thus, many people now also view art as a mere propaganda vehicle. We have feminist, Afro-American, leftist, homosexual, and other special interest "art" and "literature." Art exhibits and films are sponsored by various gay/lesbian task forces. Leftist propaganda "art" exhibits and films are sponsored by various "revolutionary" groups and their friends amongst the intelligentsia. At this point in time, much to its detriment, art has been thoroughly confused with the craft of political propaganda—not a very transcendent or uplifting craft at that! It is a craft more useful to drum-beating cranks than to thoughtful individuals. Art has been prostituted and put to the service of equal rights, affirmative action, African-American studies, and every *ism* which abounds in our now fractured, special-interest, newly-tribalized society.

Art needs its practitioners, its defenders, its lovers, and its friends as never before. Lorenzo de' Medici, call your office!

6

FREEDOM VERSUS CENSORSHIP

Persecution may shield itself under the guise of a mistaken and over-zealous piety.

EDMUND BURKE, *Impeachment of Warren Hastings,*
February 17, 1788

In his book *The Tempting of America*, Robert Bork illustrates the manner in which some judges and law professors have politicized the law in what he calls a "cultural war." This phenomenon of cultural war—reducing the disciplines to politics carried on by other means—is unfortunately not unique to the law but is effecting other areas of the life of the nation as well. In our times, various ideologically motivated groups increasingly use, in one way or another, censorship, coercion, or propaganda to limit access to ideas, literature, and the arts that they consider threatening.

The book *Huckleberry Finn* was banned in some circles when first published in 1885 because it seemed to be dangerously *against* the common racism of the day. Today there are calls by some black civil rights activists to ban *Huckleberry Finn* because the word *nigger* is used in the text. Some have called it racist.

Some fundamentalist Christian educators also wish to drop *Huckleberry Finn* from school reading lists—or worse, actually change and edit the text—to tone down what they regard as Mark Twain's antichurch, antireligious "offensive" worldview. It seems today, in our now tribalized society, that Mark Twain has trouble pleasing anyone!

People agree that Mark Twain was a great writer and that *Huckle-berry Finn* is deserving of its place in the pantheon of American fiction. Everyone, that is, except today's censors, including some who claim to be "liberal," for instance, the feminist literati. Women who would rather ignore nonfeminist literature, except when condemning it, have an aversion to prefeminist literature of all kinds, unless of course it comes from some obscure non-Western source, perhaps a Sri Lankan lesbian describing her spiritual exaltation as she contemplates her menstrual cycle!

The black leaders who want to ban *Huck*, the feminists who want to reinterpret *Huck* and all other literature, the deconstructionist critics who say it is impossible to objectively understand Twain at all, the fundamentalist Christians who want more sympathy for religion from Twain—all have one thing in common: they want to rearrange reality and history to suit their political and ideological tastes. Unfortunately, *Huckleberry Finn* is but one of hundreds of volumes of literature under attack by the ideologues in our country, from the political Left and Right and, judging by the deconstructionists' interpretations, from the lunatic asylums as well.

The New Censors

In our times, various ideologically dedicated groups increasingly use censorship, coercion, or propaganda to limit access to ideas, literature, and the arts that they consider threatening.

African-Americans

Black civil rights activists have not been subtle in putting censorious pressure on the educational system. In addition to imposing de-facto quota systems on schools to force the hiring of black professors, they have also engaged in censorship. For instance, activists pressured the Toronto, Canada, Board of Education to rule on June 23, 1988, that the novel *Lord of the Flies* was "racist and . . . that it be removed from all schools." Members of the black community complained that it denigrated blacks because the word *niggers* appeared in the text.

A number of American black Muslim leaders joined with the late Ayatollah Khomeini in calling for a ban on Salman Rushdie's *Satanic Verses*. Black groups challenged the Salem school system in Virginia

Beach, Virginia, over the use of *The Actor's Book of Contemporary Stage Monologues* because some of the dialogue in the monologues contained *racial* slurs.

Black activists also forced the removal of a painting from public display in Chicago in 1988, that offended the then black mayor of the city by portraying him in an "offensive" manner. The work was attacked

---

"In our times, various ideologically dedicated groups increasingly use censorship, coercion, or propaganda to limit access to ideas, literature, and the arts that they consider threatening."

---

as *racist* and then removed by force. Black leftists, the majority of black leaders, have also gone about quietly suppressing the views of black conservative scholars like Thomas Sowell and Glenn C. Loury, whose ideas they oppose as not reflecting their own views and *interests* on racism and welfare*ism*.

Feminists

Feminists have concentrated their censorship activities on pressuring textbook companies to remove all "sexist" and "traditional" female role models from textbooks, including reading books. They have insinuated a picture of personally approved women's roles into many textbooks at the expense of all other visions of womanhood. Feminists have also been active in a quiet, informal, hidden censorship campaign. For instance, the action of individual women editors of like mind at various major publishing companies has effectively prevented authors and scholars critical of feminism, such as Michael Levin, from publishing scholarly works that take an informed but critical view of feminist "achievements." Levin, who is professor of philosophy at CCNY, found it impossible to find a major publishing house for his book *Feminism and*

Freedom due to the individual actions of an informal sisterhood of feminists who guard the gates of access to public discourse in many of America's leading publishing houses.

When Carol Felsenthal wrote a sympathetic biography of Phyllis Schafly, *The Sweetheart of the Silent Majority,* she experienced consistent hostility leveled at her by this "sisterhood," resulting in the book being notable by its absence from many large bookstore chains, public libraries, and a whole range of magazines that would normally have reviewed a book on an important political female figure. Libraries and bookstores have many "sisters" guarding their gates. Anti-abortion literature has also often met with informal banning.

That many well-educated women tend to think the same way and exhibit a herd mentality regarding issues of the day is not surprising when one is aware of the aggressive, almost unopposed dominance that feminist theology now enjoys in academia. Typical of the results of this sort of "scholarship" is a course offered at Duke University called Interdisciplinary Studies 140, "The Great Mother: Archetype or Stereo-Type?" This course of "study" is described in the school's prospectus of course offerings (1989) as follows:

> The Jungian archetype of the Great Mother and the emerging feminist critique of the Jungian model. The dual symbolism of the Feminine as nurturing and devouring Mother, the ambivalent nature of the mother-daughter relations, the identification of woman with Eros, and alternatives to the patriarchal myth of the Mother. Readings include Jungian and feminist theories; Asian, Egyptian, and Greek mythologies; and modern fiction.

With four years of such intensive feminist indoctrination (at $18,000 to $20,000 per year!), imagine how traditional Christian ideas of truth and aesthetics, and artistic universality fare with the graduates of Duke and other schools. Unknown to them, the students in question are participating in a mammoth anti-historical, anti-Western cultural experiment that will, like the Communist experiment in Eastern Europe, eventually crash in the inevitable ruins of all extremist, ideologically authoritarian excursions. But in the meantime, this indoctrination is destroying the students' chance to enjoy a genuine education. What today's students are *not* studying is also a form of censorship. Points of view they are *not* hearing is a form of intellectual coercion practiced by those who should be encouraging them to explore their diverse intellectual cultural heritage.

Being introduced to literature and art by the politically zealous feminists and deconstructionist critics is like being introduced to sex via rape. It takes a long time to recover; literature will never be quite what it could have been for their unfortunate protégés.

To illustrate the massive revisionist campaign by feminist ideologues against the arts in general and literature in particular, Carol Iannone, in an article called "Feminism vs. Literature" (*Commentary*, July 1988), reviewed a number of works by feminist literary critics:

"That many well-educated women tend to think the same way and exhibit a herd mentality regarding issues of the day is not surprising when one is aware of the aggressive, almost unopposed dominance that feminist theology now enjoys in academia."

Sandra Gilbert, who teaches at Princeton, and Susan Gubar of Indiana University. Iannone teaches writing and literature at New York University and is editor of *Academic Questions*. In her article she notes the deliberate destruction of the concept of the transcendent universality of the arts by the radical feminists who now dominate the literary university landscape, and who, by their theories of criticism, have managed to subvert the meaning of literature. Iannone writes:

> Scarcely a single scholarly discipline now stands without its corrective feminist insurgency, and the profession of English literature is no exception. In fact, in literary studies feminism is no longer an insurgency but an ascendancy. In the words of Peter Brooks, director of

Yale's Whitney Humanities Center, "Anyone worth his salt in literary criticism today has to become something of a feminist." . . .

Professors Gilbert and Gubar's first joint work, *The Madwoman in the Attic: The Woman Writer in the Nineteenth Century Literary Imagination* (1979) was one of a number of book-length efforts to appear in the 70s aimed at analyzing literature by women as a separate category. *Madwoman* begins with a question that might seem ironic coming from a feminist perspective, namely, how did 19th-century female authors meet the monumental challenge of being both women and writers? According to Professors Gilbert and Gubar, literary "assertion" is necessarily incompatible with the habits of feminine submission demanded by "patriarchy." Therefore, the "difficult task" faced by British and American writers was to achieve "true female literary authority by simultaneously conforming to and subverting patriarchal literary standards."

Jane Austen, for example, masks beneath the serene surface of her art "a subversive critique of the forms of self-expression available to her both as an artist and as a woman." How so? By, among other things, identifying herself in her novels "not only with her model heroines but also with less obvious, nastier, more resilient and energetic female characters who enact her rebellious dissent from her culture. . . . " Similarly, in Emily Bronte's *Wuthering Heights,* Catherine's "masochistic self-starvation" during pregnancy is not the exacerbated willfulness most readers have taken it for but a protest against female fate, an "obvious response to the pregnant woman's fear of being monstrously inhabited as well as to her own horror of being enslaved to the species and reduced to a tool of the life process."

What distinguished *The Madwoman in the Attic* from previous works on the subject of literature by women was its authors' willingness to suspend normal literary standards entirely and employ a so-called "female" or "feminist" aesthetic instead. Before *Madwoman,* many would-be feminist critics had found themselves bound by the traditional criteria that they either still respected or did not yet know how to be rid of. . . .

Professors Gilbert and Gubar's second major effort, the *Norton Anthology of Literature by Women* (1985), collected writings from the Middle Ages through the 20th century. Unlike *Madwoman,* this anthology did arouse an open controversy over its methods when a living, breathing "woman writer" actually laid critical eyes upon it. Writing in the *New York Times Book Review,* the novelist Gail Godwin asserted that "the values of feminist interpretation are elevated to a *summa* at the expense of literary art and individual talents. . . ."

Miss Godwin's review provoked a flurry of angry responses. There was, predictably, no substantive disagreement with her contentions. Instead, in a letter signed by five prominent feminist critics, she was accused of "political bias" and lectured on the "illusion" of universality. "There is no universal literature," these respondents insisted, and "all of it arises from beliefs that are no less ideological for being unexamined or widely accepted as 'normal.' " Another feminist decried Miss Godwin's denial of a female literary tradition "in the face of massive and growing evidence to the contrary"; for still another, Miss Godwin's views could only be ascribed to "the resistance of a woman who is herself at odds concerning her relationship to a tradition of other women."

Of course, what specific "ideological" beliefs Miss Godwin had illegitimately propounded were not spelled out by her critics, nor was any of the "massive and growing evidence" of the female tradition actually adduced. But this did not matter. By 1985, the indignant insistence on a chimerical female tradition had obviously become a useful tool for wielding threats and subduing opponents.

Unfortunately, Professors Gilbert and Gubar are not unique in their reflections on the meaning of literature. They are part of a fashionable legion of feminist ideologues, literary critics all bent on rewriting, or should I say eliminating, the history of Western literature. Elaine Showalter, Ann Douglas, Elizabeth Hardwick, Nina Baym, and a gaggle of others have been at the forefront of the closed-minded, politicized assault.

Feminists have borrowed a page from the Marxists when it comes to aggressive tactics and the manipulation of history, theology, the arts, and literature for their own political cause. The deadly sterility of Socialist Realism that typified Stalinist art has in common with feminist literary criticism a character that is at once propagandistic, manipulative, belittling to the human spirit, and is technically incompetent though ideologically "correct." Those who are not sufficiently "sensitive" to the feminist point of view are hounded from the academy as assiduously as the K.G.B. followed dissidents, caught, and punished them under Stalin's paranoid leadership.

Fundamentalist Christians

Fundamentalist groups and individuals have also used the meat-cleaver approach to "literary criticism" as they have embarked on their own programs of censorship.

Aldous Huxley's *Brave New World* was challenged as required reading in the Yukon, Oklahoma, high school in 1988 because of the book's "language and moral content." (Thus, ironically, was dispatched by these "God-fearers" the greatest prophetic warning against a godless super-state ever penned!) *Catcher in the Rye* met the same fate at the Linton-Stockton, Indiana, High School in 1988 because the book was said to be "blasphemous and undermines morality." John Steinbeck's work fared no better. *Of Mice and Men* was challenged in the Marian County, West Virginia, schools and the Wheaton-Warrenville, Illinois, high schools, both in 1988, because the book contains "profanity." So much for great American literature.

The list of literary works under attack is unfortunately long. In 1988 alone there were more than five hundred attempts to ban books from libraries and schools across the United States. An anti-intellectual tradition in America runs deep in some quarters and is not a new phenomenon. For instance, in the Boston area, *Leaves of Grass* was banned in 1881, *Elmer Gantry* in 1929, *Strange Interlude* and *All Quiet on the Western Front* in 1930, *An American Tragedy* and *The Sun Also Rises* in 1941, and in 1950, *Strange Fruit* and *God's Little Acre*.

One common thread binds all the censors of our time: they all claim their actions are for the "good of society," or at least to liberate or protect us. Yet those who love and cherish the arts and humanities, not to mention truth, should be the first to reject claims by those who would limit human expression for some "greater good." What greater good can a society enjoy than freedom and truth? And how can freedom of expression exist in a pale, bloodless culture where not being offensive is seen as the first civic duty?

Hypocrisy abounds in the ranks of the modern "thought police." Fundamentalist Christians, who claim to worship God who endowed men and women with creative expression, can be seen vying with each other as they jockey for position on some school board to be the first in line to ban a book or boycott an "offensive" film, book, or television program. "Liberal" educators censor speech they find distasteful in the bosom of institutions committed to the free flow of ideas because they find it "sexist" or otherwise "offensive" or even "insensitive."

G. K. Chesterton once said (in an interview with the *New York Times*, November 21, 1930) that, "A puritan is a person who pours righ-

---

"How can freedom of expression exist in a pale, bloodless culture where not being offensive is seen as the first civic duty?"

---

teous indignation into the wrong things." He could well have been describing today's puritan leaders who compete in the stifling of freedom of expression.

Censorship Methods

Banned

Veronese, the great Italian painter, had a taste of censorship in his time. He had painted an enormous fresco of the *Last Supper*. Veronese peopled his painting with the biblical figures one would expect: Christ and the disciples. However, in addition he used the enormous wall space available, filling it with contemporary figures, including German soldiers dressed in the style of his time. Germany was a Reformation country and no friend to Catholic Italy or the Venetian patrons who had commissioned the fresco.

Veronese was hauled before the Inquisition for questioning as to why he had included German soldiers in a sacred work. His answer was that he had wanted to make full use of the wall space and that he had run out of biblical figures! He was ordered to paint out the offending figures—an order he ignored, saying that it would ruin his work. Instead, he simply changed the title of his *Last Supper* to *The Feast at the House of Levi*. (It now hangs in the art museum of Venice.)

At the height of the Counter Reformation, one expects such intolerance from the Inquisition. What is odd is to see twentieth-century "liberals" carrying out similar witch hunts. Today the sheer magnitude of the feminist assault on the arts may be unmatched in its brashness, even by Christian fundamentalists who have traditionally attacked freedom of speech, art, and literature, but this is not for want of trying. Mel and Norma Gabler, the founders of Educational Research Analysts of Longview, Texas, have been typical of a not very successful and crude attempt by some Christian fundamentalists to limit what some Americans can and cannot read and see. As Donald Rogers writes in his book *Banned* (Julian Messner, 1988), "These people wanted to safeguard students from what they considered dangerous ideas about sex, race, religion . . . and patriotism."

In doing so, what many students were to be safeguarded from were merely ideas at odds with fundamentalist class taste. In other words, the students were being protected from a broad view of Western culture that, ironically, had been originally informed by Christian values concerning freedom. The fundamentalist's attempted banning of *A Brave New World* serves as a good example of this outworking of a house divided against itself.

Today's ideologues are like today's corporate leaders. Corporate America complains about government restraint of business unless it is in *its* favor. Today's ideologues want freedom of speech as long as it is speech approved by *them*. They even want history rewritten to suit their taste. The earnest zealots are a legion who would ban, censor, revise, or otherwise interfere with or reinterpret ideas, culture, and history. We seem to be in a society that is descending to the level of a competition between intolerant special interest groups who all regard art and the humanities as dispensable and politics as sacrosanct.

Ironically, Christians are sometimes taking part in censorship, whether this is overt or inward guilt-ridden self-censorship. The freedom the Christian tradition brought to the men and women of the West is a direct result of the practice of biblical principles. It is no coincidence that Western society has (first in Byzantium then in the Latin West), with some regrettable exceptions, given the greatest freedom to the arts ever known in the world. This historic treasure of freedom of expression should be cherished, not squandered by allowing people with coercive or extreme views to trash art and literature, forcing it to serve their puny political ideologies.

The first duty of the artist is not to be socially conscious or to express "correct thinking." The duty of the artist is to express truth as he or she sees it. The duty of a free society is to demand, then preserve, this right, a duty that is being forgotten in our universities and that threatens our popular culture as well.

Politics

Sometimes the battle over censorship takes on overtly political dimensions. This was the case in the well-publicized debate in 1989 over the N.E.A. (National Endowment for the Arts) funding of artworks by such artists as Andres Sarrano and Robert Mapplethorpe. Both artists had produced artwork that was offensive to a large proportion of the population, including myself. Both artists' work came under attack from right wing politicians, such as Jesse Helms, and conservative commentators such as

---

"There is *no place for censorship of art or ideas in a free society.*"

Patrick Buchanan. Mapplethorpe was attacked for his photographs of vulgarly explicit homosexual subjects and Sarrano for his *Piss Christ,* a photograph of a crucifix submerged in a bottle of urine that many people, myself included, regarded as blasphemous and a very second-rate work of art, if *art* at all. Neither artists' works are particularly good, and in the case of Mapplethorpe, are often prurient.

However, be that as it may, my own view is that there is *no place for censorship of art or ideas in a free society.* I also feel that because of the necessity to preserve freedom of expression, it is a mistake to involve the taxpayer in underwriting *any* art, good or otherwise.

Attorney John Whitehead, president and founder of the Rutherford Institute (a religious civil rights organization), writes concerning government funding of art.

Funding art places the government in the untenable position of placing its financial weight behind ideological propaganda. A free government must in principle be evenhanded and nondiscriminatory in what it supports. If a free government, then, funds one form of art, it cannot logically deny another form. (Private correspondence with the author, February 9, 1990)

As Whitehead points out, the government has no business in the art business at all. But as long as the government *is* in the misbegotten business of underwriting artwork, then the government should not censor artwork based on what it interprets as morally good or bad. To do so means that it is drawn unwittingly into the censoring ideas in a free society.

Censorship invites reciprocity in public discourse by those who resent the censorship of what they would otherwise approve or tolerate. For example, Nicols Fox writes in *The New Art Examiner* (Summer 1989) in an article entitled "NEA under Siege":

Irony abounds in this affair. In the current supermarket atmosphere that characterizes Christianity, an extraordinary diversity of beliefs is not only tolerated but supported by those who call themselves Christians. Those who rise in outrage against the *Piss Christ* raised not a whimper of protest against the long-running Praise the Lord Club (PTL) heresy. Jim and Tammy Bakker were allowed to preach and practice, in the name of Christianity, a doctrine of pure materialism, a gospel of goods and getting and an eternal life in the hot tub—the antitheses, to be precise, of Christ's Sermon on the Mount.

Freedom of expression does not imply that everyone must approve all that is said or done. It is, I think, legitimate to boycott an artwork or a media presentation as our exercise of freedom. As a believing Christian, I am careful about what images I wish to absorb. For instance, I did not see *The Last Temptation of Christ*. To me, my image of the Lord Jesus Christ is too precious to risk by seeing images of Him that are detrimental to an Orthodox understanding of His life and work. However, the fact that I did not want to subject myself to such images is not to say I wished to deprive Martin Scorsese of the right to make his movie or that it was a badly made movie much as I might have hated the experience of watching it.

In a free society, there is a legitimate role for protesting things, including art, that we find distasteful. There is a difference between *boycotting* something and *censoring* it. It is inappropriate for the government to spend the tax dollars of its diverse citizens to underwrite art that its citizens will find distasteful. However piecemeal, censorship is not the answer. Freedom is—freedom *from* government censorship or support, and freedom to make moral-artistic choices in a free market of free ideas.

Methods vary when art is censored: It can be banned outright, as Jesse Helms suggested as he attacked the funding of certain kinds of artwork, or it can be censored by giving it a false, antihistorical interpretation that imposes a present-day ideology on the minds of the young and impressionable, as feminist scholars are doing when they indoctrinate the semiliterate and inexperienced with their crude political ideas. I believe both methods to be inappropriate, in fact and in spirit, within a free society.

Labeling

Besides naked attempts to ban books, art, and films, there are other ways in which artistic and intellectual expression is being systematically intimidated in our society. There are unspoken but clearly understood parameters now effectively limiting what can or cannot be said in "right-thinking" company. Black civil rights advocates have become experts in using the label of *racist* to intimidate any person, even a fellow African-American, who offends them, however legitimate their point of view. Some Jewish groups use the label *anti-Semitic* as a bludgeon with which to silence all adverse opinions concerning the state of Israel or other questions of particular interest to Jews. Feminists have become past masters at condemning as *sexist* those who dare to oppose them in their political machinations. And in some circles, the fear of being labeled *homophobic,* is enough to silence those who challenge the orthodoxy of belief of some gay rights' task force.

Many speakers whose views are not congenial to the "right-thinking" leftists who dominate American campuses, have been literally driven from the podium by the vicious behavior of those bent on denying them the right to be heard. Supposedly liberal institutions, such as Harvard, have specialized in accommodating the rantings of these latter-day Brown Shirts in the very heart of educational institutions once dedicated to free speech.

Islands of Repression

Chester E. Finn, Jr., who served as Assistant Secretary of Education from 1985 to 1988 and is now professor of education and public policy at Vanderbilt University, writes in an article entitled "The Campus: An Island of Repression in a Sea of Freedom" (*Commentary,* September 1989) about the rising tide of "liberal" intolerance in our universities:

> Two weeks before the Supreme Court held that the First Amendment protects one's right to burn the flag, the regents of the University of Wisconsin decreed that students on their twelve campuses no longer possess the right to say anything ugly to or about one another.
>
> Several months earlier, the University of Michigan adopted a six-page "anti-bias code" that provides for punishment of students who engage in conduct that "stigmatizes or victimizes an individual on the basis of race, ethnicity, religion, sex, sexual orientation, creed, national origin, ancestry, age, marital status, handicap, or Vietnam-era veteran status." (Presumably this last bizarre provision applies whether the "victim" is labeled a war hero or a draft dodger.)
>
> Not to be outdone by the huge state schools, a number of private universities, like Emory in Atlanta and Stanford in California, have also made efforts to regulate unpleasant discourse and what the National Education Association terms "ethno-violence," a comprehensive neologism that includes "acts of insensitivity. . . ."
>
> Constraints on free expression and open inquiry do not, of course, depend on the adoption of a formal code of conduct. Guest speakers with controversial views have for some years now risked being harassed, heckled, even shouted down by hostile campus audiences, just as scholars engaging in certain forms of research, treading into sensitive topics, or reaching unwelcome conclusions have risked calumny from academic "colleagues." More recently, students have begun to monitor their professors and to take action if what is said in class irks or offends them.
>
> [The] additions to the formal and informal curricula of American colleges and universities, like the behavior codes and anti-harassment policies the institutions are embracing, are invariably promulgated in the name of enhancing "diversity" on campus. That has become the

chief purpose of present-day affirmative-action hiring and admissions policies, too. . . . In recent months, I have run into several outstanding young (white male) political scientists who are finding it impossible to land tenure-track teaching posts at medium- and high-status colleges because, as one of them wryly explained to me, their scholarly strengths lie in the study of "DWEMs." When I confessed ignorance of the acronym, he patiently explained that it stands for "Dead White European Males." Had they specialized in revolutionary ideologies, the politics of feminism and racism, or trendy quantitative social-science methodologies, they could perhaps have transcended their inconvenient gender and mundane color and have a reasonable shot at academic employment. But to spend one's hours with the likes of Aristotle, Machiavelli, Hobbes, and Burke is to have nothing very important to offer a political-science department today, whatever one's intellectual and pedagogical accomplishments. . . .

Diversity and tolerance, evenhandedly applied, are estimable precepts. But that is not how they are construed in the academy today. Nor do the narrowing limits on free expression lead only to penalties for individuals who engage in "biased" talk or "hostile" behavior. They also leave little room for opinion that deviates from campus political norms or for grievances from unexpected directions.

Literature

Great literature comes from the desire to write and write well and expresses the artist's love of life and interest in his or her fellow creatures.

> **"Those who politicize art and historical interpretation are, I believe, the enemies of humanity."**

Politics, in contrast to art, serves a worthy but distinctly different purpose. Its power to move human action is directed to more temporary questions.

The "politics" of the artist's work in question is often more in the eye of the beholder than in the artwork itself. Thus by one generation, *Huckleberry Finn* is labeled as scandalously anti-slavery, by another as scandalously anti-black. Perhaps tomorrow someone will say it is anti-Jewish, homophobic, or anti-environmental! But what was Mark Twain writing about? And how do we honor his efforts? First, I believe we study his life and the context in which he wrote. Deconstructionists and feminists aside, it is not beyond the realm of possibility that we can, through a little research, place Twain and other authors' intentions in rather clear perspective. We should also be humble enough to recognize that we are not so uniquely "enlightened" in our day as to be altogether different from our forbears. We share with them a universal human experience of life that *transcends* time, space, race, *and* gender.

So what was Twain up to? It seems to me that he was writing a book about the adventures of a boy; a story he infused with the timeless warmth of human companionship that never changes. Huck's sense of morality, his tenderness towards those in distress; Jim, the runaway slave's loyalty and compassion; the tawdry scenes about the exploits of the Duke and the King, punctuated by moments of Huck's unexpected virtue: these are attributes universal to the human character. These are the themes of all people's lives. These are the attributes of humanity that interest Twain, Dante, and Homer. These are the *common* bonds that span *all* time, history, races, and the sexes. That is not to say that there is no subtle, social satire in *Huckleberry Finn*; there is. But real art transcends mere politics.

The very fact that people *do* have common bonds holding them together alarms the special interest "scholars" of today. Those, such as feminists, "gays," marxists, some black activists, and fundamentalist Christians, who wish to segregate themselves from the rest of humanity have a vested, if unconscious, interest in destroying our common artistic and human heritage. They all have the same agenda: to separate little segments of the human race from the rest of humanity and to claim these "tribes," these unfortunates as their own, to be "led" whither the particular demagogues in question wish to lead them for their own political, sociological, or theological purposes. Integration, of the kind that Martin Luther King Jr. advocated, is the concept furthest from their minds. Today's ideologues work tirelessly to erect new barriers between races, creeds, and the sexes. This new racism and sexism is alive and well in the bosom of the "liberal" establishment.

Art is one part of the glue that binds people together. Is it any wonder that in this fractured age of special interest politics that art has been under attack or prostituted to become mere propaganda? Those who politicize art and historical interpretation are, I believe, the enemies of humanity—a humanity that the church fathers understood to be unified into one body, progressing from darkness toward the light of progress under God's hand of divine providence.

Re-Editing—Even Babar!

Every imaginable artistic expression is now threatened by the new censors and their "politically correct thinking." One might think that a children's literary classic would be safe. Not so. In the 1981 edition of Random House publisher's *Babar's Anniversary Album,* six Babar stories from the 1935 edition of *Babar's Travels* have been edited in order to omit stories and illustrations which might offend some contemporary tastes. In this case, an episode was edited in which Babar and the queen of the elephants, Celeste, are attacked by a tribe of cannibals while stranded on an island. No doubt this hatchet-editing was done in service of some hypothetical standard of what black America, or at least the self-proclaimed leaders of the welfare plantation, are supposed to want children to read. As a result of this kind of tampering multiplied in hundreds of incidents, we find a sort of United Nations blandness creeping into even children's books and textbooks, in which "right thinking" is seen as more important than literary integrity, personal opinions of the author, history, or truth. It amounts to little more than censorship by the bland, for the bland, of the bland, and produces books that offend and interest no one. And since reality is deliberately distorted, the reedited books tell lies about the intent of the author or history. This is a tragedy, and in the case of the Babar books and other children's books, ridiculous as well. We are becoming a nation of pale "equal opportunity" bureaucrats when it comes to our ideas of what is appropriate in art. We are becoming slaves to "politically correct" thinking.

By Default

There is another form of censorship rampant in our culture—the trivialization of knowledge through television.

In *Amusing Ourselves to Death*, Neil Postman points out that as we moved from the rational linear thought promoted by the typographical age into the television age of irrational emotionalism fed by images, we have unwittingly rendered information trivial. Thus our access to knowledge is, in a way, censored by the trivialization of information presented via television. Postman writes:

> Television clearly does impair the student's freedom to read, and it does so with innocent hands, so to speak. Television does not ban books, it simply displaces them. . . .
>
> There could not have been a safer bet when it began in 1969 than that "Sesame Street" would be embraced by children, parents and educators. Children loved it because they were raised on television commercials, which they intuitively knew were the most carefully crafted entertainments on television. To those who had not yet been to school, even to those who had just started, the idea of being *taught* by a series of commercials did not seem peculiar. And that television should entertain them was taken as a matter of course. . . .
>
> We now know that "Sesame Street" encourages children to love school only if school is like "Sesame Street." Which is to say, we now know that "Sesame Street" undermines what the traditional idea of schooling represents. Whereas a classroom is a place of social interaction, the space in front of a television set is a private preserve. Whereas in a classroom, one may ask a teacher questions, one can ask nothing of a television screen. Whereas school is centered on the development of language, television demands attention to images. Whereas attending school is a legal requirement, watching television is an act of choice. Whereas in school, one fails to attend to the teacher at the risk of punishment, no penalties exist for failing to attend to the television screen. Whereas to behave oneself in school means to observe rules of public decorum, television watching requires no such observances, has no concept of public decorum. Whereas in a classroom, fun is never more than a means to an end, on television it is the end in itself. . . . (pp. 142–144)

While there are many who would debate some of Postman's conclusions, I, for one, find his argument convincing. How else can we explain the trance-like stupidity which stamps the faces and actions of a legion of "teenagers" (people ranging from age twelve through fifty!), who populate the nether world which is the product of so much of our media age?

The M.P.A.A.

At times, attempts to censor lead to ridiculous hair-splitting. I became aware of just how silly trying to "rate" art or media for public consumption can become when I first encountered the ratings board of the Motion Picture Association of America. The M.P.A.A. are the people who rate movies as G, PG, PG13, R, and NC17 for the American film-going public.

One of my movies was once threatened with an X (before the "X" rating was dropped in favor of the "NC17") for "violence" until I agreed to cut a scene by three seconds to eliminate a slap that the villain, a man, gave a girl, the heroine in the movie. That year, 1985, the fashion was to ban "violence against women" in movies (at the same time feminists were actively pushing for women to assume combat roles in the military). The M.P.A.A. had no problem with the many remaining scenes in which men were killed. Having cut the offending slap, I was rewarded with an R, thus the picture was then "releasable." (Major studio pictures routinely are awarded PG ratings for movies that have a great deal more violence in them than many a small, independent movie like mine. In status-conscious Hollywood, studios carry clout that small, independent producers do not possess.)

To give a movie an X for whatever reason was to effectively ban a film. An X-rated picture was automatically considered a *porno movie* whether it even had any sexual content or not. (Mine had none.) An unrated or X-rated movie could not get a good general release. Many newspapers will not carry advertising for X-rated movies, no matter what the film's actual content. The M.P.A.A. forces almost half of the independently produced movies to make some content changes to get the rating needed to have a chance at a successful release. Depending on what's "in" and what's "out," the "suggested" changes can range from the trivially absurd, as in the case of my movie's offending slap, to the substantial, in which case whole scenes are cut, often rendering the story of the movie unintelligible.

Sometimes, as in our AIDS-conscious times, *sex*, at least of the "unsafe" variety, is out, sometimes it is *violence,* sometimes *language,* sometimes simply material that is subjectively considered *offensive.* This offensiveness can be anything that the M.P.A.A. expects will generate heat from groups ranging from homosexual lobbyists (no homophobic humor) to feminists (no girls to be slapped—unless in combat roles, I suppose) to fundamentalist preachers (no anything) to African-Americans (no black stereotypes).

Yet no one is satisfied by this system. Some find it permissive; others, like me, find it silly. Yet, perhaps the capricious nature of the M.P.A.A. serves useful notice to us about the nature of censorship. Imagine the chaos in other fields of the arts that more heavy-handed censorship would cause, if the resulting confusion among moviemakers, because of the rather mild coercion of the M.P.A.A., is any indication. Certain things do not lend themselves to legislated regulation. Art is one of them. Politics is not the solution to all human problems. Recourse to the law is not the only or the best way to settle differences of opinion. "Sensitivity" cannot be demanded by law in a society that wants to also have free speech.

Self-Censorship

Extreme self-imposed censorship because of false guilt feelings is just as much a tragedy among some believing Christians as official censorship. Self-censorship based on false guilt retards and shrinks life in an anti-human, anti-Christian way.

Those who wish in our present day to interpret reality for us, whether they are right-wing fundamentalist preachers, television executives as mindless as their victims, feminists, leftist ideologues, or African-American leaders, are miserable misers of life's experiences who would starve our spirits and give us a ration of thin ideological gruel, "right thinking," and trivial "sensitized" nonsense for subsistence.

The impulse to censor the arts and humanities on the part of so many men and women of modest personal achievements is suspect. As G. J. Nathan wrote, "Criticism is the art wherewith a critic tries to guess himself into a share of the artist's fame" (*The House of Satan,* 98).

Life is far bigger, far more diverse, glorious, dangerous, and complex than today's various censors would have us believe.

In the first century A.D., Seneca wrote that "the times will come when our successors will wonder how we could have been ignorant of things so obvious." One only hopes that these words will not be fulfilled

---

"Those who wish in our present day to interpret reality for us . . . are miserable misers of life's experiences who would starve our spirits and give us a ration of thin ideological gruel, 'right thinking,' and trivial 'sensitized' nonsense for subsistence."

---

by our own grandchildren looking at what we did as we passively abandoned the arts and humanities to the cranks. And one also hopes that one day soon the arts and humanities will be restored to their rightful place, and that they will once again be treated with deference, even love.

The Offense of Truth

The greatest works of art are often offensive to someone. They are not made to suit the tastes of blacks, whites, males, and females as if the human race were no more than a tribalized collection of political action committees. Nor is art made to please a multiracial panel of experts. Instead, it is created to express one person's vision of reality—the artist's! To force the art of the past into the straitjacket of contemporary, interpretive, ideological crusades is to squander the birthright of all human beings, male and female, black and white. The glory of art is that it can and does transcend passing fads, political squalls, and ideologies. The glory of freedom of speech is that people, even artists and authors, have the right to be wrong. And, yes, even the right to be racially, politically, or chauvanistically "insensitive."

Art is the language of the soul, not the servant of political action committees, "right-thinking" ideologues, or trendy editors. To revise history in general and art in particular from an exclusively modern point of view is the height of arrogance. Such a revision attempts to put words in people's mouths and attribute political thoughts and motivations to them from our perspective rather than from their own.

The feminist, deconstructionist, and Marxist interpretations of the arts and humanities are arrogant attempts to steal from the people of the past their legitimate place in history and their voice. This rewriting of history is a censorship of ideas, just as surely as book-burning. Fundamentalist book burners use matches and gasoline; feminists, et al., use symposia and journals. Both forms of censorship are motivated by a desire to control, even legislate reality. Not satisfied with ruining the present, these people also want to destroy the past, like worms boring into some irreplaceable, priceless illuminated manuscript. They are parasites, living off the very culture they are destroying.

Christians should realize that censorship is a two-edged sword. As the deliberate mischievous misuse of the concept of the separation of church and state (that has been abused to sometimes keep evangelical and fundamentalist Christians out of the political arena or social debate) should demonstrate, we should be wary of giving a government or other semiofficial bodies, like the A.C.L.U. or the M.P.A.A., the power to censor ideas, art, or political debate. As Robert Brustein wrote in an article entitled "The First Amendment and the N.E.A." (*New Republic,* September 11, 1989), "If you are not prepared to protect bad speech, you are in a poor position to protect the good." The law that can stop the expression of ideas or art we find offensive can also, and probably will at some point, be used to prohibit *religious* expression that many people now find *offensive, sexist, homophobic, obscene, anti-Semitic,* or a perversion of the separation of church and state.

This is not to say that *all* human expression of *any* idea or *all* visual content is sacrosanct. There is no reason that child pornography should be legal. There is no reason that prostitutes should be coerced into being sodomized while pictures are taken to sell in "adult" bookstores. There is no reason that in a free country standards of behavior cannot be set down in law to prohibit the victimization of those used in the manufacture of pornography. This is not censorship; this is simply the application of the ancient common laws against pedophilia, homosexual acts, prostitution, and sexual coercion that amounts to rape. Such laws to protect the innocent should be vigorously enforced.

Nevertheless, there will be gray areas. There always are. Yet a great deal of the *production* of pornography clearly involves the victimization of people, which is not a gray area. Civilization has the right to protect itself from the criminal abuse of sexuality. And sensible men and women of good will should work hard to see that this legitimate protection of innocence does not then overstep its bounds and become a form of coercion. Sadly, by the very extremism that so many Christians and feminists have embraced in denouncing *all* nudity, violence and "language" in legitimate art and media, they have unfortunately disqualified themselves in this debate at the very time when their voices might be very usefully raised in the defense of virtue.

Censorship, in contrast to protecting the victims used in the pornography trade, is a pandora's box of unintended consequences that in the end affects everyone with something to say. The recent trend, by those who dislike someone's free speech, to resort to sueing them under R.I.C.O. statutes (Racketeer Influenced and Corrupt Organization act), which were designed to curb mob activities (not free speech or freedom of assembly), show the level to which some malicious people with an ax to grind will sink. The call for censorship, on the part of some people, is the result of well-intended, utopian, romantic notions of how we can "do good" to people by protecting them from some ideas. On the part of others, as the illegitimate use of R.I.C.O. tactics against pro-life groups and others illustrates, it is a deliberate attempt to silence free speech and to circumvent the right to assembly.

A Tradition of Freedom

Turgot, the eighteenth-century statesman and economist, is sometimes considered the father of modern secularism. Yet even he, in his famous first address at the Sorbonne University in Paris in 1750, lauded Christianity above all else for its unique role in giving freedom to slaves, serfs, bondsmen, and others, including women, who, prior to Judaism and Christianity, had been in pagan bondage. Turgot, building on this idea of Christian freedom, went on to extol the virtues of progress in science and the arts as *dependent* on that freedom. He frequently commented on the indispensability of individual freedom to inspire progress in art and science.

Edward Gibbon, author of *The Decline and Fall of the Roman Empire,* also recognized in the Christian West "the system of arts and laws and manners which so advantageously distinguished . . . the Europeans and their colonies."

Adam Smith was a believer in freedom and, as is less known today, in Christian altruism of the kind taught him by his great Glasgow professor, Francis Hutcheson, who himself was a devout follower of Shaftesbury. It was Shaftesbury's compassionate work to regulate child labor that began to humanize the harsh face of the early industrial revolution. Smith, contrary to the misinformed belief of our times, was deeply sensitive to the needs of the poor. Yet he believed that *freedom* was the answer to their needs; it would liberate economic resources chained by regulations and custom and enrich the whole of society. Smith's point of view has been largely vindicated as noted by historian Paul Johnson (also a believer in freedom) in an article entitled "The Capitalism and Morality Debate" (*First Things,* March 1990).

Voltaire, another French thinker not known for his sympathy to Christianity, in his *Philosophical Letters* asserted that America was an improvement over free, merry old England and that the Quakers of Pennsylvania had created "that golden age of which men talk." In the writings of all these men, we see the reiterated fact that the West in general and America in particular has a great tradition of freedom—a tradition being eroded by the new censors and the trivialization of knowledge by the media.

Censorship, the twin brother of propaganda, is the tool of despots, of ideologues, of ayatollahs, of fanatics. However, there are more subtle forces at work hindering our ability to reason freely. For instance, television, the drug of a profoundly stupid society, creates a climate of silliness which becomes a form of self censorship. It is insecure people who reach for the censor's pen and people of flaccid intellect who reach for their television remote controls. Censorship of ideas, direct or indirect, should have no place in the community of Christians who have the truth as their spiritual foundation.

Christians should stand against propaganda, even religious propaganda. We should uphold the image of God in people; the image that is creative and free, even free to make wrong artistic choices. We should stand against censorship in all its various and subtle forms, including that of amusing ourselves to death. The culture may be moving away from rationality, but there is no reason we should follow.

Legislating Reality

Restricting the freedom to communicate through art and media produces the same bad results as restricting economic freedom. Socialism is a failure because government cannot legislate economics successfully. By arranging an economy ideologically from the top down, a government stifles productivity and creativity, hurting rather than helping people's economic prospects. The gross failure of every redistributive, socialist-communist economy proves this (not to mention the gross failure of America's socialized, centralized, public educational system). In this respect, art is similar to commerce. You cannot edit artistic impulses

---

"Stagnation of the human spirit is the bitter fruit of all forms of censorship."

---

through censorship and the whims of elites—whether they be black leaders, feminists, homsexuals, fundamentalists, or communist governments—and get good results. Stagnation of the human spirit is the bitter fruit of all forms of censorship. It is true that people do, at times, abuse their freedoms economically and artistically. The existence of pornography shows this to be true in the media, as do shady business dealings on Wall Street in commerce. However, censorship of the economy or art is not ultimately the answer to sin: Truth is. As history has demonstrated, it is worth the risk of abuse to have the massive benefits of freedom—freedom that Christians can use as they speak the truth as they understand it.

7

NAKED AGAIN

*Nothing is so chaste as nudity. Venus herself, as she drops
her garments and steps on to the model-throne, leaves behind
her on the floor every weapon in her armory by which she
can pierce to the grosser passion of man.*

GEORGE DU MAURIER, *Trilby*

I n our time, the question of the use of nudity and violence in art has
divided Christians of goodwill, not to mention countless Christians
of ill will who, like the poor, seem to always be with us.

The Bible

The Bible is not only the Word of God, divinely inspired to give people
understanding of the way of salvation, but is also a literary work, a work
of art. Descriptions of nudity as well as extreme violence are found in
profusion in the Bible. From the story of the Garden of Eden to such
instances as Noah's youngest son looking on his nakedness, to the
Levite's concubine who was cut in twelve pieces and distributed to the
twelve tribes of Israel at God's command, to the account of David cutting off two hundred Philistine foreskins, to the graphic sexuality of the
Song of Songs, to Christ's often violent imagery in His parables, we
find realistic, factual, literary descriptions of sex, nudity, and violence in
the Bible. We also learn that God has used violence and people's sexual
behavior, even immoral behavior, to shape history, to punish the wicked,
to chastise, and to build up His people.

God, evidently, is not worried by any ratings board, not to mention the maintaining of polite niceties. When it comes to His own literary work, even His action in history, God's attitude seems to be, let the chips fall where they may. The Bible is many things, but it is certainly *not* suitable "family entertainment." The Bible would probably not be sold in any "Christian bookstores" if it was perceived as merely a book to be thoroughly read rather than as a *religious* devotional work.

As Christians we look to the Scriptures for moral teaching. From their study we can conclude that the Bible seems unafraid of flesh and deals openly with nudity and violence. Historically, the church has not always been as unfriendly toward flesh as some fundamentalists are in our own times. Historian and scholar Etienne Gilson shows there was not a lack of awareness of the physical aspects of the individual in the church of the Middle Ages.

> One of the surprises in store for the historian of Christian thought lies in its insistence on the value, dignity, and perpetuity of the human body. The Christian conception of man is almost universally taken to be a more or less thoroughgoing spiritualism. . . . But to the no small scandal of a goodly number of historians and philosophers the contrary turns out to be the fact. St. Bonaventura, St. Thomas Aquinas, Duns Scotus, I will even say St. Francis of Assisi himself—one and all were men who looked benignly on matter, respected their bodies, extolled its dignity, and would never have wished a separate destiny for body and soul. (As cited by Robert Nisbet in *History of the Ideas of Progress* [New York: Basic Books, 1979], 80-81)

The Historic Vacuum

Pascal wrote: "Men never do evil so completely and cheerfully as when they do it from religious conviction" (*Pensées,* Sec. XIV, no. 895). Fundamentalist mischief to the arts by pious men and women has been great. "I fear this iron yoke of outward conformity hath left a slavish print upon our necks" (Milton, *Prose Works,* Vol. II, 97).

It is the exercise of a peculiarly Protestant arrogance that ignores church history and holy tradition and assumes that as we look for answers to moral problems, we are alone before God, armed only with our own subjective reading of Scripture and our puny consciences. The fact that in their wisdom, countless faithful churchmen, Orthodox, Roman Catholic, and Protestant, through generations before and after the Reformation found nothing intrinsically offensive about nudity and violence

---

"The Bible seems unafraid of flesh and deals openly with nudity and violence."

---

in art is instructive, at least to those who regard themselves as part of the historic church.

Unfortunately, in addition to ignoring church history, few Christians seem to understand the importance of the *context* in which something appears. Thus they are left with a few, inadequate, simplistic rules, which are not necessarily biblical or aesthetic, by which to judge art.

There is no single rule that covers the question of aesthetics in art, including violence and nudity. Each work must be judged individually and in its context. The situations portrayed by a Christian in the arts are of merit if they accurately portray the truth of a subject honestly and properly in its context. Reality *is* tragic, violent, bloody, and evil, not to mention sublime and beautiful.

Those seeking to work as Christians in the arts will explore their own way haltingly and with little absolute certainty in these areas. They will get almost no help from today's evangelical let alone fundamentalist Christians. If they seek guidance, they will have to look elsewhere. The historic church beckons.

Nudity in Art

By consulting various sources (including James Hall's most helpful *Dictionary of Subjects and Symbols in Art* [New York: Harper and Row, 1974]), we learn that the response to nudity in art by people in all periods of Western history has varied from time to time. Yet the nude human figure has always been a dominant, if not the dominant, subject in the visual arts. Both in pre-Christian Western history and the Christian era, nudity in art has been common.

Orthodox, Roman Catholic, and Protestant teaching and tradition has approved some nudity in art at some times and disapproved of it in some contexts at others. The context in which nudity was used and the subject being portrayed have been the determining factors in judging its appropriateness. Usually when objections to nudity have arisen, our own fundamentalistic, pietistic times being the exception, it has been over its perceived misuse, not over nudity itself.

Pliny, in his *Natural History* (36:20-22), writes that a nude statue of Venus was eagerly purchased by the islanders of Cnidus, having been rejected by the islanders of Kos. From this example we learn that some Greeks of the classical period accepted nudity in art and some did not. To the Romans, nudity symbolized various things: shame in some cases, poverty in others, and beauty in yet others.

In the Old Testament, the graphic eulogy of the female body and its sexuality in the Song of Songs seems to contradict another sentiment of Hebrew modesty expressed, for instance, in Jeremiah 13:26: "So I myself have stripped off your skirts and laid bare your shame!" (NEB).

However, descriptions of nakedness and nudity run through the Scripture, sometimes as a description of fact, such as the nakedness of Adam and Eve, other times as a metaphor for vulnerability. There are one hundred and four verses in the Old and New Testaments in which the subject of nakedness is a central theme. In addition to which, there are countless other frank allusions to sexuality, nudity, and violence as part of biblical history.

The best preserved Byzantine and early church art in Western Europe is found in the form of the magnificent mosaics in Ravenna, Italy. There in the Cathedral Baptistry one finds a startling mosaic of the baptism of our Lord. St. John the Baptist stands above Christ on a rock to His left. Christ stands in the transparent River Jordan as a dove hovers over Him. Christ is portrayed nude. He stands facing forward, His body uncovered and naked as were the bodies of all believers who were baptized in the early and Orthodox church. This mosaic was completed about the year A.D. 400. An early fifth-century work in an official building of great importance, it certainly tells us that nakedness and shame were not considered the same thing by the bishops of the early church.

Far from Ravenna being some back water, it was the Byzantine capital of Europe. The Baptistry was commissioned by Archbishop Neone not more than three hundred years after the generation who saw Christ alive.

To the Christian church of the Middle Ages, nudity in art presented four different aspects. The first, *nuditas naturalis*, was personified in nude paintings of Adam and Eve before the Fall or the nakedness of the

---

"Orthodox, Roman Catholic, and Protestant teaching and tradition has approved some nudity in art. . . . The context in which nudity was used and the subject being portrayed have been the determining factors in judging its appropriateness."

---

many martyrs such as St. Sebastian—graphic nudity and extreme violence combined to illustrate his bloody and painful death. Nudity was also used in portraying the resurrected at the Last Judgment. Nude bodies were often used in a purely decorative way, for example consider a personal favorite of mine, the many nude figures carved into the marble pulpit in Orvieto's cathedral. These were all seen as worthy and good uses of nudity by churchmen and laymen alike. Far from frowning on such artworks, the church itself commissioned and displayed them.

The second category of nudity, as accepted by the church of the Middle Ages, was *nuditas temporalis*—nakedness understood in a figurative or allegorical sense. It symbolized the absence of worldly goods, either as a result of a misfortune, as with Job, or by saintly choice, exemplified by St. Francis of Assisi and the penitent Mary Magdalene. The same idea of naked purity is expressed by Milton in his descriptive line, "In naked beauty more adorned" (*Paradise Lost,* Bk. IV, l. 713).

The church understood nudity in art to also be *nuditas virtualis*—the third aspect of nudity that represented a quality of sinlessness in daily life, as in the nakedness of Truth. Finally, there was *nuditas criminalis*.

This represented, in art, the ancient sins condemned by the prophets and was embodied by representations of the pagan gods and goddesses as well as the devil himself.

In the late thirteenth and fourteenth centuries, the Western church began to commission nude figures of the virtues, such as naked Truth painted standing next to robed Mercy, illustrating Psalms 85:10. The church also sponsored art containing nudity in scriptural themes to which it properly belonged—Massaccio's *Adam and Eve* in the Carmen Chapel in Florence or the figures in Giotto's *Last Judgment,* for example.

The human figure, naked and robed, was the keystone to Renaissance art in Catholic Italy *and* northern Protestant painting as well. From the first works of the Renaissance by painters like Cimabue, Giotto's teacher, to Leonardo da Vinci's anatomical studies in the late Renaissance, the human body was perceived as good, *the* fit subject for study, portrayal, and enjoyment. The human body was the basic model for all drawing, draftsmanship, and sculpture. To remove the nude figure from art of that, or indeed any period, would be to remove the very basis of all figurative artwork in Western art history.

The Florentine philosophers and theologians during the Renaissance taught that of the two aspects of love, divine and earthly, divine love was superior. To express contempt for the things of this world, they believed that divine love should be symbolized by a naked woman. This reflected the Orthodox heritage in which, for instance, St. Mary of Egypt was venerated for her willingness to wonder naked in the desert for forty years in renunciation of worldly goods. Earthly love was portrayed as a clothed woman, richly dressed and bejeweled.

During the Renaissance in Italy, the Western church's stated attitude toward nudity in *secular art*—art not commissioned by the church itself—was ambivalent. However, we see in Cosimo de' Medici—the greatest patron of the church *and* the arts of the fifteenth century—a man who, as well as supporting San Marco and the religious works of Fra Angelico, also commissioned in 1440 the nude sculpture of *David* by Donatello. This was the first sculpture since Roman times made to be seen "in the round," from all sides. It was unashamedly nude, with no implication of sin or disgrace in its biblical narrative portrayal of a young, innocent male body.

Later, the portrayal of nudity in religious art, not other art, was condemned by the Council of Trent (a council not accepted by the Eastern Orthodox Church as valid and thus not a universal, ecumenical council) except for religious subjects that specifically demanded it—Adam and Eve, the Last Judgment, and so on. The Council of Trent notwithstanding, many individual churchmen continued to commission art containing nudity in nonsanctioned subjects, for instance, in Carreggio's frescoes in

---

"In the Protestant north of Europe, nudity was not perceived as wrong *per se* by most churchmen until the post-Victorian pietistic times which foreshadow our own."

---

the Camera di San Paolo at Parma, Italy (1518), which were the apartments of the abbess of a convent, or the decoration of the Farnese Palace in Rome by the Carvacci brothers for Cardinal Odoardo Farnese at the turn of the sixteenth century.

In Spanish art, redolent of a lingering Islamic repression, nudity is more rare. Goya, of course, painted beautiful nudes such as his *Maja nue*, as well as religious subjects, portraits of royalty, and so forth. He also portrayed the sins of *nuditas criminalis* in his etchings and paintings of nightmares, witchcraft, and other horrors.

In the Protestant north of Europe, nudity was not perceived as wrong *per se* by most churchmen until the post-Victorian pietistic times which foreshadow our own. And even in the era of Queen Victoria, we find a great deal of nudity in ninteenth-century British art of Blake and others. Though the prudish Ruskin, as the executor of Turner's estate, is said to have burnt a whole portfolio of Turner's "indecent" drawings!

Long before the advent of the Victorian era, Lucas Cranach, the German painter and a devotee, friend, and follower of Martin Luther (even the godfather to Luther's children), painted various nude subjects including his famous *Adam and Eve*. Luther was very fond of Cranach and his paintings and commissioned him to paint portraits of himself and his wife. In this context it is also worth noting that Luther was unashamed of his own sexuality. We have his letters to a friend describing, in what would be seen by today's timid Christians as unhealthy and ribald terms, the pleasures of his marriage bed, complete with allusions to the pleasure he took in penetrating his wife and other robust, earthy sexual references.

Albrecht Dürer, a devout believer and an early follower of Luther, portrayed nude subjects in his etchings, including his biblical illustrations such as *Adam und Eva,* as well as many other works. For instance, his strong pen-and-ink drawings, including *Ein Frauenbad* (The Women's Bath), *Der Mann mit dem Lowen* (Man with a Lion), and his *Das Grobe Gluck* (Nemesis), all portray nude men or women. Dürer also used mythological figures in his work—his nude *Apollo* for example—thus echoing the Italian Renaissance interest in the classics. His anatomical studies in human proportion also mirror a scientific-artistic interest similar to Leonardo da Vinci's. In fact, his female nude study of *Figur aus der Proportionslehrer* (female proportions) uses the same configuration as Leonardo's famous male proportion study that has since become a worldwide symbol of humanity.

In his own writing, faith, and work, Dürer seems to have seen no conflict between his nude studies, his classical mythological studies, his biblical subjects, and the various portraits he did of religious figures of his day, including one of Erasmus in 1521. Like most believing Christian artists throughout history, Dürer felt no tension between his deep, personal faith in Christ and his artwork. The wide-ranging choice of subject matter also tells us that Dürer fully understood all of life to be God's and rejected the division of life into *secular* and *sacred,* as if the *sacred* were more important. Dürer pays as much loving attention to a painting of a rabbit crouching next to a dandelion as he does to his portrayal of Christ at the *Last Supper.*

Rembrandt and the other Dutch seventeenth-century masters painted nudes fairly frequently. Rembrandt's nudes include those of his wife, who, like all artists' wives, often served as his model. Rembrandt, as a devout Reformation Protestant, is typical of his time in his use of nudity. Rembrandt's paintings mirror reality in a down-to-earth way that speaks of an artist at peace with who he is and with a knowledge of the world and its fullness. His interests, like Dürer's, ranged beyond biblical themes to the ancient classics, for example, in his red chalk drawing of *Cleopatra* as she seductively presents her breast to the serpent. In *The Anatomy Lesson of Professor Tulp*, Rembrandt paints not only the portrait of the students and the professor but a very dead cadaver, the tendons of its left arm dispassionately dissected. In *The Rape of Ganymede*, a child is plucked aloft by an eagle. The fearful infant is urinating as he looks desperately for help. In *The Holy Family* we see Mary in a darkened interior. She holds her breast out for the infant Jesus to suck. An old woman looks on tenderly. Joseph, in the background, goes about his day's work as a carpenter. The total, unromantic realism of the scene speaks of the historicity of the Christ child as Rembrandt saw Him. In *Susanna and the Two Elders*, all the voyeuristic lust of the ages is written on the faces of the two "dirty old men." One is tugging at the drape of a young, naked, and vulnerable girl—innocence contrasts sharply with the jaded elders as they use their status and respectability to try and coerce her into giving them sexual favors. Using a wide choice of subject matter, Rembrandt and Dürer are typical of the artists of the Reformation era who were devout Protestant believers.

In our own times, Christian artists, such as the Roman Catholic mystic Rouault, have painted nudity, and Jewish artists like Marc Chagall, have also used the nude figure delightfully. Today, thoughtful evangelical Christian artists, like Steven Hawley and Edward Knippers, continue to use the nude figure, male and female, as a central part of their work.

In retrospect, we can see in church history that an outright ban on all nudity is extremely rare. And a ban on violence in art, or even the idea that portraying violence could be morally bad in itself, is almost totally unknown in church history outside of our own time. The questions discussed by serious and informed men and women have always been about what nudity is appropriate to what subject in what context. Classical Greece and Rome, the Roman Catholic Church, and later the Protestant reformers seem not to have shared the attitude of modern pietists that nudity or violence in art is itself wrong in *any* context. Thus the evangelicals and fundamentalists of today are out-of-step with the traditions of the historic church, Catholic and Protestant, on the one hand, and with the explicitly descriptive passages of Scripture, such as the Song of Songs or the crucifixion of Jesus, on the other hand. (In this light, one wonders what an art department at some evangelical or fundamentalist Christian college that forces its students to draw models in bathing suits is doing, other than making an unintended joke at the expense of both art and Christianity.)

The Christian artist who wants to proceed with his or her painting, writing, sculpture, film, drama, and photography can therefore feel secure that present-day fundamentalist-evangelical hostility in some quarters concerning nudity and violence in art does not represent the wisdom of the ages, the Bible itself as a work of literature, or for the most part, church history and tradition. The precedent set by the great Christian artists who once dominated Western art history tells a very different story, one of freedom of expression.

Christian artists today must be as courageously creative in pursuing their work in the face of evangelical, fundamentalist opposition as was Michelangelo, who got around the problems of a temporary church ban on anatomical studies by striking a deal with the prior of Santo Spirito in Florence. He was secretly allowed to dissect corpses in the cloister in exchange for carving a crucifix for the canny prior!

Pornography

Pornography, like the poor, will always be with us. In the pre-photographic age, the Romans sometimes used their fresco paintings to portray pornographic images. For instance, in one fresco in Pompeii, one can see a man with a huge penis masturbating into a cornucopia of fruit—pretty obvious stuff, even if excused as a homage to fertility! Yet no one in his right mind confuses this crudely fashioned "art" with the serious and sublime classical sculpture of Greece and Rome. In our own times, we can see a vast difference between sexuality being sold as sinful pornographic titillation in some so called "adult" magazines and serious works of art. Common sense *should* tell us this.

There is a clear difference apparent to many people, though perhaps not to many A.C.L.U. lawyers or fundamentalists, between voyeurism and aesthetic nudity in art. Some evangelical-fundamentalists have called all nudity in art *pornography*. An unintended consequence of such overstatement has been the fact that by such absurd conjecture they have made it virtually impossible to stand against *real* pornography in any meaningful and effective way. Those who cannot see the difference between Michelangelo's *David* and an X-rated video tape in which two women are copulating with one man and an animal cannot really be taken too seriously. Crude, sexually abusive images produced for people

> **"Those who cannot see the difference between Michelangelo's *David* and an X-rated video tape . . . cannot really be taken too seriously."**

to masturbate on are of an entirely different kind than those of art works. This may be a difficult concept to write into law in a free society, but, I believe, it is one that is not impossible to grasp for the average person.

False Piety

Typical of the fundamentalists' attitude toward nudity in art is a passage from a famous "Spirit-filled" television evangelist's biography in which he speaks passionately of the changes he made in his domestic life after his conversion to the Christian faith from "secular humanism." In one passage he explains to the reader how he and his wife removed all traces of *secular* and *evil* things from their lives. The list of "sins" they renounced in favor of a closer walk with God included a reproduction of a certain nude painting he had in his house. The painting was a Modigliani, the beautiful if over-reproduced *Nu Assis* (seated nude) painted in 1914 by the famous Italian artist. Modigliani is one of the greatest painters of the early twentieth century, a painter whose work was limited exclusively to the human figure, which he painted in very expressive works distinguished by their purity of line. Modigliani's lifetime of work was thus dismissed as "sinful" by an evangelist whose personal, "sanctified" taste, as exhibited in his multimillion dollar university and

television studio complex, runs to neo-colonial, Williamsburg-type structures on the scale of airplane hangars—buildings that look as if the
Daughters of the American Revolution had commissioned Albert Speer
to design a funeral home!

Conclusion

It is no accident that Christians throughout history, from early fourth
century Ravenna to our own times, have been drawn toward portraying
the human figure. God's most complete and beautiful earthly creation
has, by Christians, been understood to be men and women—men and
women with beautiful, ugly, lumpish, or sublime, but always interesting,
souls and bodies.

"And the LORD God formed man of the dust of the ground, and
breathed into his nostrils the breath of life. . . . And the LORD God
caused a deep sleep to fall on Adam, and he slept; and He took one of
his ribs, and closed up the flesh in its place. Then the rib which the
LORD God had taken from man He made into a woman, and He brought
her to the man" (Genesis 2:7, 21–22). God, who could simply speak a
word and create matter from nothing, chose instead to *sculpt* the human
form from clay and bone. Is it any wonder that His image-bearers, His
children, have inherited His love of sculpting the human form?

8

TRUTH VERSUS PIETISM

*The advances in human rights of which we Americans can be
justly proud (however partial they might yet be) can be traced
to the fact that they were successfully advocated as a
development out of the traditions which long predate
the founding of the American republic.*

DAVID NOVAK, *First Things*

*The Holocaust was, in largest part, the consequence of ideas
about human nature, human rights, the imperatives of history
and scientific progress, the character of law, the bonds and ob-
ligations of political community.*

RICHARD JOHN NEUHAUS, *First Things*

There are two opposite traditions present in the history of the
church and in the lives of individual Christians today that coexist
and often seem to overlap. One tradition has produced, in various forms,
the positive fruits of Western culture—the art and commerce that the
whole world, including today much of the once communist world, is
trying to imitate in order to produce Western-style freedom and prosperity in their own nations. The other tradition has produced a lasting leg-
acy of human, social, and artistic problems.

The first tradition declares Christian teaching to be truth, the explanation of existance itself. This tradition holds that God is the Lord of all
reality and that He created all that is visible and invisible. Because of
this, we live in an orderly universe that can be rationally investigated
and understood through science and the arts.

The second tradition holds Christianity to be a mere *religion,* a form of psychotherapy. People who hold this second view only believe Christianity is true in the sense that it is helpful personally or gives religious answers to certain psycho-spiritual questions. This tradition declares that life is divided into compartments, some "spiritual," others not; it does not affirm reality as one indivisible whole.

These two traditions run through all church history in all denominations, including present-day evangelical-fundamentalist and charismatic Protestant denominations. These two competing traditions are also apparent in the historical and current Roman Catholic and Orthodox churches. These two worldviews vie for our attention, for the direction of the historic church, and the direction of individual Christians' lives. Many Christians are unaware that their faith is informed by one of these points of view.

For our purposes here, I shall call the first tradition *Truth* and the second tradition *Pietism.* The faith of most Christians is not clearly informed by either Truth or Pietism but is in some way a mixture of the two. However, the results and quality of the Christian's individual life depend on which worldview he or she espouses.

The battle between Truth and various forms of Pietism has taken many historical twists and turns. This is not a history book, nor am I a historian. However, it is appropriate that we should look at one specific historic confrontation between the forces of Truth and those of false spirituality. Thus, it can serve as an example of the wider, more prevalent conflict between Truth and Pietism we are examining now.

What better guide than G. K. Chesterton and what better example than Saint Thomas Aquinas. Chesterton examines the ideas of Aquinas as he combated the false spirituality of Manicheism. In his time, people who held this belief divided reality into the "spiritual," thus important, and the "temporal," the unimportant, in much the same way as today's pietists emphasize irrationality and "spirituality" at the expense of reality and Truth. The Manichees followed a pseudo-Buddhist "Christianity" that regarded the physical-natural world of matter as the source of evil and the spirit world as the source of good. Therefore, they hated the flesh and exalted the spirit, thereby, in fact, denouncing God's created reality and Christ's redemption of it.

If we wanted to put in a picturesque and simplified form what he [Aquinas] wanted for the world, and what was his work in history, . . . we might well say that it really was to strike a blow and settle the Manichees. . . . What is called the Manichaean philosophy has had many forms. . . . But it is always in one way or another a notion that nature is evil; or that evil is at least rooted in nature. . . .

Now it was the inmost lie of the Manichees that they identified purity with sterility. It is singularly contrasted with the language of St. Thomas, which always connects purity with fruitfulness; whether it be natural or supernatural. . . .

In this sense St. Thomas stands up simply as the great orthodox theologian, who reminded men of the creed of Creation, when many of them were still in the mood of mere destruction. . . . (*Saint Thomas Aquinas* [New York: Doubleday, 1956; first published by Sheed and Ward, 1933], 102-111)

If this all has a very familiar ring, it is because this age-old battle never changes, only the players do. Those who regard Christianity as a

---

"The faith of most Christians is not clearly informed by either Truth or Pietism but is in some way a mixture of the two."

---

mere spiritual experience and those who regard it as Truth are still locked in combat today as they were in Saint Thomas Aquinas' time.

Truth

The tradition of Truth affirms life as a whole; it sees reality as a whole. There is no sacred and no secular—all of creation is God's. Indeed the affirmation of orthodox Christian truth is the affirmation that all of creation is to the glory of God and that the physical world is not "lower" than the spiritual. In fact, the physical world of flesh and nature has been re-created by the fact that Christ came *in the flesh*. God's commands are not merely moral commands affecting our moral standing before Him; they are also the instructions provided by God telling us how we, as His creatures, work best. God's law is not only a means of identifying what is right and wrong as it is commonly understood, but also as a question of what works and what does not. From the point of view of Truth, this makes sense. If God has created reality, then He will know how it functions.

In creating human beings, God made a biological "machine," similar to the rest of the biological world, which He then infused with a conscious mind and soul. (Something like the computer robot creature in the movie *Short Circuit*: "Number five *is* alive.") We are biological machines that can choose: Choose to read God's instruction manual and live by it, or choose to disregard it and pay the price of self-destruction.

Law and creation have the same source: God. They, like spirituality and the physical world, are part of reality that God has made. God's law as expressed in the Scriptures, His instruction, is not a series of pious sayings; it is a set of practical rules by which our biological, mechanical bodies and our nonbiological spirits can function and prosper.

The Results of Truth

If Truth *is* true, then it *should* work to whatever extent it is understood and obeyed. This has practical applications. For instance, the prosperity and freedom in the West, which the world envies and seeks to copy, is not merely an economic system that came into being by mere accident. Whether they know it or not, what the underdeveloped countries wish to copy are the fruits of Truth rooted in the ideas of Christian teaching.

As Michael Novak, (author and George Frederick Jewett Scholar in Religion and Public Policy at the American Enterprise Institute), wrote in *Commentary* (September 1989) in an article entitled "Boredom, Virtue and Democratic Capitalism":

> Democratic capitalist societies are rooted in certain spiritual values without which they could scarcely have been imagined, let alone have come into existence.
>
> From the beginning the claim was made of democratic capitalist societies that they were built to the pattern of "the system of natural liberty." The implication was that such a system would belong to all

humans, wherever they might be. It would be adaptable to local cus-
toms, histories, traditions, and cultures, provided only that these
opened the institutional ways to universal human capacities for reflection and choice—in politics, economics, and the realm of conscience
and culture. The system was not designed for Jews or Christians only,
for Anglo-Saxons or Frenchmen; it was designed for all human beings.

This claim is not forfeited by the historical fact that the insights and
practices which originally led to the developments of the necessary

---

"The tradition of Truth affirms life as a whole; it sees reality as a whole. There is no sacred and no secular—all of creation is God's."

---

institutions arose first in lands deeply shaped by the teachings of Judaism and Christianity. That democratic capitalism was embryonically
realized first in such lands was, of course, "no accident." Judaism and
Christianity are, in an important way, religions of history and conse-
quently, religions of liberty. . . .

It was out of such beliefs that the words of Thomas Jefferson in the
Declaration of Independence ultimately flowed: "We hold these truths
to be self-evident: That all men are created equal; that they are endowed by their Creator with certain inalienable rights; that among
these are life, liberty, and the pursuit of happiness; that to secure these
rights, governments are instituted among men, deriving their just powers from the consent of the governed; that whenever any form of government becomes destructive of these ends, it is the right of the people
to alter or abolish it, and to institute new government, laying its foundation on such principles, and organizing its powers in such form, as to
them shall seem most likely to effect their safety and happiness."

As Novak writes, ideas, in this case theological ideas, bear results in
the practical world. While a Judeo-Christian tradition leads to certain
economic and political results, these benefits can also be shared in part
by non-Christian societies because reality *is* one, and men and women
are made in God's image, whether they acknowledge Him or not. Just

as the rain falls on the just and the unjust, so even those who are *not* followers of Truth still live in a cause-and-effect world, in which, through trial and error if not through a commitment to theologically accurate ideas, they can benefit from and work with the natural order of things. Nature and history carry a cause-and-effect message from God. Revelation is a short cut to that message.

But the opposite can also be true. Cultures that have known the orthodox Christian Truth can choose to abandon their principles. As the West abandons Christian descriptions of reality and Truth and follows other ideas, it, too, could regress and join the so called Third World. Those who lift their voices in the chant "Ho, ho, Western culture has got to go!" are attacking not only Western culture but Truth, and the progress, prosperity, and freedom that follow from that Truth. They are committing spiritual, artistic, and economic suicide.

Truth does work, and its opposite—lies and deception—leads to destruction and chaos. The human race is not divided along ethnic or racial lines; it is divided between those who follow true ideas and those who do not.

Western culture is not *the* Truth, but to the degree it has succeeded in producing a system that feeds, clothes, and defends its citizens and upholds their civil liberties, the West has benefited from a *belief* in the principles of Christian Truth. (A fact amply demonstrated by a growing body of scholarly literature, including: P. T. Bauer, *Equality, the Third World, and Economic Delusion* [Cambridge, MA: Harvard University Press, 1981]; Julian Simon, *The Ultimate Resource* [Princeton, NJ: Princeton University Press, 1981]; Warren T. Brooks, *The Economy in Mind* [New York: Universe Books, 1982]; Michael Novak, *The Spirit of Democratic Capitalism* [New York: Simon and Schuster, 1982]; Paul Johnson, *Modern Times* [New York: Harper and Row, 1983]; and Robert Nisbet, *History of the Idea of Progress* [New York: Basic Books, 1980]).

Christian principles of freedom, individual accountability, the rule of law, humanity, and compassion have produced magnificent results applied to political institutions and economic practice, a fact underscored again by the many church-led revolutions against communist tyranny of recent memory. The people of what was once Communist East Germany, Romania, Poland, Hungary, and Czechoslovakia have struggled to replace the yoke of the superstate and communist dictatorships with Western and Christian institutions. Thus, while some in Western academia, the media, the "knowledge elite," continue to be enamored of socialist ideas, the people of the world, when given any chance, beat a path to the door of the West and its *religious* institutions for guidance.

The West they seek to emulate is the West founded on the concept of biblical Truth and the tradition of the historic church, which from its

---

"Pietism is a process of constantly looking inward and searching for spiritual feelings. Pietism seeks to obey not only the Laws of God, but also a host of petty rules lifted up as 'absolutes.'"

---

earliest days forward has produced a stream of enlightened and humane institutions and philosophies that have deeply affected the lives of average people within its sphere of influence. From the Orthodox church of Byzantium with its many orphanages, hospitals, and charitable institutions, as well as its stand against abortion and slavery, to today's democratic principles of freedom, the history of Christianity is the history of human progress toward the light.

Pietism

Those whose Christian opinions are informed by Pietism regard life as a moralistic quest for spiritual experience. For Pietists, the results are unimportant if only the motivation is correct. It is the emotional experience that concerns them, not the mind or the soul. Pietism is a process of constantly looking inward and searching for spiritual feelings. Pietism seeks to obey not only the Laws of God, but also a host of petty rules lifted up as "absolutes." Content, truth, and logic take second place to experience, fervor, and rule-keeping. In this regard, Pietism is in perfect tune with the times.

Because of the premium often put on feelings and emotion by pietists, those in this frame of mind may seek out many experiences which are fundamentally irrational, thus anti-Christian. These experiences will help them, they hope, in their rather desperate quest for a religious "high," the emotion and *feelings* they imagine to be holiness. Thus, "worship" often becomes hysterical. Mood, feelings, and "sensitivity" replace real discourse about ideas and true, mystical, spiritual content. Since the pietist looks to emotion to validate his or her faith, almost anything that heightens that emotion is perceived as good. This has opened pietists to abuse and false teaching in large numbers. This has also led to many pietists becoming disillusioned as things get out of hand, or when the promised results from their "walk with the Lord" fail to materialize. Many finally abandon their faith altogether, throwing out the baby with the bath water. This is why one meets so many ex-fundamentalists and hedonistic pagans who were raised in "charismatic" or evangelical homes that were cut off from the faith and practice of the historic church.

Chesterton writes of the destructive trend toward pie-in-the-sky Pietism in the church as he related Aquinas' battles in his day. Aquinas locked horns with a certain wrong-headed gentleman by the name of Siger of Brabant:

> Siger of Brabant said this: the Church must be right theologically, but she can be wrong scientifically. There are two truths; the truth of the supernatural world, and the truth of the natural world, which contradicts the supernatural world. . . . In other words, Siger of Brabant split the human head in two . . . and declared that a man has two minds, with one of which he must entirely believe and with the other may utterly disbelieve. . . .
>
> St. Thomas [by contrast] was willing to allow the one truth to be approached by two paths, precisely *because* he was sure there was only one truth. Because the Faith was the one truth, nothing discovered in nature could ultimately contradict the Faith. Because the Faith was the one truth, nothing really deduced from the Faith could ultimately contradict the facts. (*Saint Thomas Aquinas,* [New York: Doubleday, 1933], 84-91)

In our time the same battle rages; St. Thomas Aquinas would be at home in the modern church. He would recognize in the "liberals," those who, like Siger of Brabant, want to have Christianity be religiously "true" though not true in the objective or historic sense. And he would do battle with some more conservative thinkers like Allan Bloom who think Christianity "useful" but not true. Aquinas would also hear—in the charismatic movement and the evangelical trend toward psychological

---

"Those Christians who have subscribed to the pietistic view of life can be recognized by the fact that they are driven by an inner, guilty need to 'Christianize' all they do, to somehow make it 'holy' in order to justify it."

---

well-being at the expense of Truth—echoes of the anti-reality Manicheism he labored so long to combat.

Pietism gives people a fractured reality, one in which the physical world, the body, the arts, economics, the sciences, the humanities, and sexuality are believed to be evil or at least lower than the spirit world. A world in which fact is seen to be at war with religious experience. One can see a guilt-ridden motivation at work in the actions of many who have abandoned their "secular" talents in favor of "serving God"—an attitude embodied in the "I used to be a night club singer but now I'm a missionary" variety of Christian. Many a missionary and missionary's child has suffered because of the tragic mistake of pursuing the missionary calling out of some false sense of guilt—guilt fostered by a protestant church that pushes people into "the Lord's Work" as if it were something special, separate, and better from "ordinary" life. Thus, pietists develop a hierarchy of values in which "spiritual" activities and full-time religious service are seen to be on a higher plain than "ordinary" life and activities. This is contrary to the teachings of Scripture in

which we are instructed to imitate Christ who came *into* the real world
of sinners to offer salvation.

Those Christians who have subscribed to the pietistic view of life
can be recognized by the fact that they are driven by an inner, guilty
need to "Christianize" all they do, to somehow make it "holy" in order
to justify it. For them, for something to be worthwhile, it must be *made*
to mean something spiritual or at least to *feel* spiritual. In our day, this
impulse is seen in everything from bumper stickers, which Christianize
cars; and Christian TV, which Christianizes the airwaves; to *The Christian Mother Goose*, a book that simultaneously Christianizes literature
while bastardizing it. Sadly, all of these efforts miss the point of Christian faith. That is, that God has redeemed all His creation through Christ
and that we do not need to trivialize this truth in order to be "spiritual."

Garbage of the Soul

The little Bible verses stuck on refrigerators, the bad Sunday school
illustrations, the feeble and bland feminized Sunday school texts of the
"be nice to everybody" variety that evangelical "Christian" publishers
specialize in, the many church programs, the lack of interest in the arts
or their propagandistic misuse, the many little rules that have been
added to God's sensible instructions, the "niceness" of so many Christians when toughness of mind is called for, the lack of courage, the laws
of God that have been abandoned, the strange tangents churches go off
on, the obnoxious bad taste, the predominance of hair-sprayed charlatans
who lead churches, the cultic overtones of the evangelical-fundamentalist movement, the lesbian-feminist inroads into the liberal denominations, the feminized wimps who pass for men in the evangelical world,
the insular closed minds, the easily shocked sensibilities of the middle
class and their taboos, the harsh rules of the fundamentalist churches,
the increased New Age emphasis on inner healing and so called counseling, the "Liberation" theology—these things, and the list could go on,
are related in one way or another, to the unnatural division of life into
religious versus secular, sacred versus rational. The chaos in many
churches is the result of removing normal, rational, historic, Christian
tradition and biblical standards, by which to judge the world, and replacing them with the "spiritual" standards of pseudo-Manacheism. The pi-

etists have created a desert where a garden should be growing. They are tragically wrong.

The Real World

Reality is one and it is all God's. There is *nothing* intrinsically more spiritual about saving a soul than filling a tooth. And there is nothing more spiritual about feeding the hungry than taking a walk with your children.

Creation, art, marriage, work, the historic Orthodox Apostolic church, the family, and all human activities have intrinsic value as does all of nature. These things have value in themselves because they are part of God's creation. It includes physics, biology, nuclear science, cinema, feeding the poor, the Eucharist, and housekeeping! God's reality includes everything, though we are told that He does not approve of everything we choose to do.

"The pietistic need to 'Christianize' reality indicates a worldview that does not fundamentally understand or believe that reality is *already* God's and that historic Christianity is truly Truth."

God has an abiding interest in mankind; Christ came to us as "The Lover of Mankind." Easter morning gives new meaning to the value of reality and all human life—meaning that modern faith-in-faith Pietism can only muddy.

The pietistic need to "Christianize" reality indicates a worldview that does not fundamentally understand or believe that reality is *already* God's and that historic Christianity is truly Truth.

We do not need to "Christianize" breakfast by memorizing a daily Bible verse. Breakfast is already God's. We do not need to "Christianize" our refrigerator by putting a small piece of plastic on it with a magnetic backing, stamped with the words, "Jesus Loves You." We do not need to feel compelled to put our children in Christian schools in order to "Christianize" academic subjects. A good school with good teaching about truth is what is required. The truth that encompasses math, physics, and history is part of the same reality as the truth about what happened historically one afternoon when Jesus fed five thousand bewildered people. And the truth about genuine liturgical historic Christian worship is in contrast to the modern "worship" of make-it-up-as-you-go-along protestantism.

Results

To bring the subject specifically back to our culture, the humanities, the media, and art, good art, like good science, describes the truth of a small or large part of reality without regard to maintaining the respectability of the artist. The fit subject for Christian art, therefore, is *reality*. This is the concept that, applied to art, science, the humanities, and political thought, created Byzantium of Orthodox Christianity out of which came the West that the world envies.

Democracy, free markets, freedom of expression, modern medicine, modern science, literature, art, and scholarship follow in the wake of belief in Christian Truth and the practice of that belief. An understanding of the fact that we live in an orderly universe created by an orderly, personal God and that all of His creation is open to us creates different results from Hinduism, Animism, Marxism, or other "religions" that do not describe reality truthfully. If we throw away the instructions, we pay the price. The rusting Mercedes Benz by the side of some post-colonial road symbolizes more than merely a return to tribalism. Philosophy and popular mechanics are related. Closer to home, the failure of government programs that seek to legislate away sin in our super-welfare state also bears testimony to the failure of Socialist and other ideas that run counter to the nature of people—their need for charity, forgiveness, motivation, and self-discipline.

The economic and human ruin spawned by the expansion of Big Government, often under the guise of a secularized mock-"religious compassion," has shown that even in the West there is no immunity from bad ideas translated into misguided programs. Aid to dependent mothers, many affirmative action programs, a host of social welfare programs, and now child-care legislation, all have produced bitter, unintended consequences. Worse, such programs attempt to impose a vision of "right thinking" from the top down, often at the instigation of special interest groups that have a vested interest in some particular government program. (For instance, child-care professionals seek to, by law, eliminate the competition of informal child-care providers, such as relatives or "the lady down the street," so that they can establish a state-imposed monopoly on child care in the name of providing "safe" facilities.) In the West, as it has lost its Christian-Jewish religious-philosophical bearings, such utopian, often jaded Statist ideas that are replacing religion as the core provider of values in our culture, are hard to resist.

Nature abhors a vacuum, and as Western men and women forget or reject the robust truths of Christianity and Judaism, the moral vacuum will be filled by government programs and the creeping socialist dependency of the welfare plantation which is increasingly presided over by professional cranks who call themselves "civil rights" activists. An extension of government into every area of life, including the arts, has become the menace of the free West. Big government has become the secular religion of a society that is abandoning the historic Christian church.

The Vacuum

Others besides Christian apologists have noticed the decline in discourse in the Christian community, a decline caused by Christians imitating the general culture as it abandons rationality in favor of "experience." Yet, it was not always so. Once, to be a Christian was not to automatically be irrational. Pietistic Christianity was *not* always the norm. As Neil Postman writes concerning the shift from rationality to Pietism in the church:

> Unlike the principal figures in today's "great awakening"—Oral Roberts, Jerry Falwell, Jimmy Swaggart, et al.—yesterday's leaders of revivalist movements in America were men of learning, faith in reason, and generous expository gifts. . . .

The doctrinal disputes among religionists not only were argued in carefully drawn exposition in the eighteenth century, but in the nineteenth century were settled by the extraordinary expedient of founding colleges. It is sometimes forgotten that the churches in America laid the foundation of our system of higher education. Harvard, of course, was established early—in 1636—for the purpose of providing learned ministers to the Congregational Church. . . . The Presbyterians founded, among other schools, the University of Tennessee in 1784, Washington and Jefferson in 1802 and Lafayette in 1826. The Baptists founded, among others, Colgate (1817), George Washington (1821), Furman (1826), Denison (1832) and Wake Forest (1834). The Episcopalians founded Hobart (1822), Trinity (1823) and Kenyon (1824). The Methodists founded eight colleges between 1830 and 1851, including Wesleyan, Emory, and Depauw. . . .

In the eighteenth and nineteenth centuries, religious thought and institutions in America were dominated by an austere, learned, and intellectual form of discourse that is largely absent from religious life today. (Neil Postman, *Amusing Ourselves to Death* [New York: Viking Penguine, 1985], 54–56)

That Western countries, with a history of commitment to Truth, even if abandoned for some time now, are not completely riddled with graft, corruption of every kind, tyranny, State theft, agrarian disaster, complete stagnation in the arts and culture, viciously inhuman institutions, and filthy water is not a fluke. It is not to be explained by some simple North-South equation or mere resource availability. As P. T. Bauer has argued so eloquently in his book, *Equality, the Third World and Economic Delusion* (Cambridge: Harvard University Press, 1981), that Mozambique, Angola, and Cuba are qualitatively different from Greece, Spain, France, Switzerland, or Holland is not an accident of race, natural resources, colonialism, or luck. The vast differences between nations has everything to do with the application of theological, secular, and religious *ideas* by the people of those countries. It has everything to do with the commitment to the Truth and its practice. It has to do with arranging societies along lines that fit the way mankind and the physical world really functions, instead of creating societies based on inaccurate moral or scientific theories into which people are coerced.

The success of the West and those nations that have imitated it, or like Japan were forced to adopt Western ideas at gunpoint, is the result of and in direct proportion to the understanding of the fact that reality works a certain way. The acceptance of Christianity at some point in a nation's history, or at least rational, Judeo-Christian thought patterns about cause-and-effect reality, is the key difference between the Western *developed world* and the *third world*. Even the vague memory of Christian thought has proved a better basis for society than non-Christian philosophy and tyranny. The West is not only different from the rest of the

---

"Even the vague memory of Christian thought has proved a better basis for society than non-Christian philosophy and tyranny."

---

world, it is measurably better—a fact that may be disputed by leftist ideologues in Western universities and the media, but is driven home by the millions who seek refuge in the West from the "other traditions," cultures, and non-Christian religious ideas.

The West has been at its most horrible when it has abandoned its own humane Christian traditions and embraced "other ways" of seeing things, as Germany did when led by the rabidly anti-Catholic, anti-Jewish madman, Hitler. Or as the Iberian Roman Catholic Church did in being influenced by the harsh Moslem views of the Arabs, who conquered, then dominated much of Spain.

In Fernand Braudel's classic history *The Mediterranean (And the World in the Age of Philip II)*, he writes about how Spain inherited more than buildings and irrigation techniques from the Moslems.

> One of the problems of the Mediterranean, and one of the causes of its traditionalism and rigidity, was that . . . newly acquired land remained under control of the wealthy. . . . Spain had inherited [from the Moslems] the labor force of *fellahin* [serfs and slaves]. . . . Spanish masters cared for . . . them in the same spirit as they would their livestock and

exactly as they were to protect their slaves in the New World. ([New York: Harper and Row, 1966], 75)

As the example of Spain shows, even Christian societies can either depart from the Truth or be corrupted by alien ideas.

Japan: An Object Lesson

Even the imitation of the *imitation* of the Christian West produces better social results than a philosophy that bears no resemblance to the Truth as embodied in Christian ideas. For instance, Japan's present prosperity can be directly traced to the borrowing of Western ideas in the 19th century and later to the new political-philosophical shape that General Douglas MacArthur *forced* on Japan from 1946 to 1952.

The Japanese, in 1946, may not have believed in Jesus of Nazareth, but they did come to believe in Douglas MacArthur. MacArthur, who was a believing Episcopalian Christian, very deliberately applied Christian ideals to the radical restructuring of post-war Japanese society. Toshikazu Kaze, the Japanese diplomat who was charged to report directly to the Emperor, speaks of his first impression of MacArthur: "Here is a victor announcing the verdict to the prostrate enemy. He can exact his pound of flesh if he so chooses. . . . And yet he pleads for freedom, tolerance, and justice. For me who expected the worst humiliation, this was a complete surprise." But to those familiar with the history of how Christians treated the lands they conquered during the one thousand year Byzantine empire, MacArthur's magnanimity would have been no surprise. For just as the Orthodox Christians sent missionaries north to convert Russia and Armenia, MacArthur's interest in Japan was not obliteration but change.

MacArthur spoke of the Japan he faced: "If we do not devise some greater and more equitable system, Armageddon will be at our door. The problem basically is theological and involves a spiritual recrudescence and improvement of human character that will synchronize with our al-most matchless advances in science, art, literature, and all material and cultural developments of the past two thousand years. It must be of the spirit if we are to save the flesh." At another time the general said he would like to be remembered as, "One whose sacred duty it became, once the guns were silenced, to carry to the land of our vanquished foe the solace and hope and faith of Christian morals."

And that was exactly what MacArthur did. Later, in the controversy surrounding the end of the Korean War, some Americans forgot what the grateful Japanese remembered: that one man had saved them by the power of ideas—ideas of freedom, women's rights, economic empowerment, free markets, human rights, and the sanctity of the individual. All of these are Christian-Western attributes, totally foreign to the Japanese in philosophy and practice until MacArthur imported them.

Arthur M. Schlesinger quoted a Japanese as saying, after the Emperor, Hirohito, had renounced his divinity, "We took MacArthur as the second Jesus Christ."

Roger Baldwin of the American Civil Liberties Union commented as he left an interview with MacArthur in Japan, "Why he knows more about civil liberties than I do!"

The *New York Times* observed, "MacArthur's administration is a model of government. . . . He has swept away an autocratic regime by a warrior god and installed in its place a democratic government."

MacArthur wrote the new Japanese constitution. William Manchester tells us, "He wrote his first memorandum on the subject, starting: 'Four points for a Constitution.' Later the General wrote, "It is undoubtedly the most liberal constitution in history." Under MacArthur's messianic influence, Japan's national income passed prewar levels within five years. MacArthur understood the power of Western ideas as perhaps no other twentieth-century political-military leader besides Winston Churchill. MacArthur said, "The more missionaries we can bring out here . . . the more occupation troops we can send home." Ten million Bibles were imported on his order, and he said that he had contributed to "the greatest spiritual revaluation the world has ever known." By this he did not mean the acceptance of Christian doctrine itself per se, though two million Japanese did convert, what he was referring to was the acceptance of Western democracy, which he understood to be a spiritual manifestation of the Christian ideas of Truth. Later, MacArthur said that the struggle for Asia lay between imperialistic communism and Christian democracy, an idea sadly vindicated by the boat people of Vietnam and the silent dead of Cambodia that followed in the wake of the anti-Christian communist advance and wholesale Western retreat from Asia after the Vietnam debacle.

MacArthur's influence in Japan provides a unique example of just how well ideas rooted in Christian belief work on a practical level, even when people are not individually believers. (The quotations on Mac-Arthur are cited from *American Caesar,* by William Manchester [New York: Little, Brown and Co., 1978], 452-551.)

The story of MacArthur in Japan is one of the shining examples of Christian statecraft, an example of culture-building without parallel since St. Constantine and the early missionary thrusts of the first to fourth centuries into the remains of the Roman Empire and beyond.

Conflict

Since the seventeenth century, the time of the so-called Enlightenment, Christians have had conflict thrust upon them by a group of secularized thinkers and artists who reject all forms and manifestations of Christian tradition. These thinkers' spiritual grandchildren continue to shape our culture, including our artistic culture, to this day.

Much of our post-Enlightenment art seems to have been directed against our own Western society. The same is true of the anti-Western nature of many twentieth-century scholars' work. Thus, for example, the stranglehold of secularism on our universities continues to this day. This secularism often takes the form of a leftist, "New Age," or "Green" extreme environmentalist ideology that rejects the West as the despised "sexist," "chauvinistic," "colonialistic," "polluting" stepchild of now hated Judaism and Christianity.

By rejecting Christian truth, many Western secularists have now come to reject their own civilization founded on that truth. It is no wonder, then, that feminists seek to rewrite not only literature and art history but even the Bible. It is no wonder that militant homosexuals seek ordination in the church. It is no wonder that feminists wish to make us refer to God as "She." They understand where our culture came from even if many pietistic Christians do not. "Ho, ho, Western culture has got to go!" is no idle refrain. It comes from those who understand the full meaning of the historical reversal implied in this slogan—the abolishment of the Christian tradition. The fact that there are even some people who espouse views that they call "evangelical feminism" or "catholic homosexuality" tells us that the power of the modern world and its fashions seem to be greater than the power of churches to resist temptation at times.

Those who have rejected Christian faith have rejected the democratic foundation of Western society itself—a society distinguished from

---

"By rejecting Christian truth, many Western secularists have now come to reject their own civilization founded on that truth."

---

other cultures by its ideas of progress and social advancement based on ideas that are divinely inspired and non-negotiable.

History and Progress

Robert Nisbet (Albert Schweitzer Professor of Humanities Emeritus at Columbia University and scholar at the American Enterprise Institute for Public Policy Research) has written the seminal study on the relationship of the idea of progress and its historical foundation entitled *History of the Idea of Progress* (New York: Basic Books, 1980).

His summary in the epilogue of his book is instructive. His remarkable analysis is essential reading.

> What is the future of the idea of progress in the West? Any answer to that question requires answer to a prior question: what is the future of Judeo-Christianity in the West? For if there is one generalization that can be made confidently about the history of the idea of progress, it is that throughout its history the idea has been closely linked with, has depended on, religion or upon intellectual constructs derived from religion. . . .
>
> It was belief in the sacred and the mythological that in the beginning of Western history made possible belief in and assimilation of ideas of time, history, development, and either progress or regress. Only on the basis of confidence in the existence of a divine power was

confidence possible with respect to design or pattern in the world and in the history of the world. . . .

But it is absent now, whether ever to be recovered, we cannot know. (pp. 352–356)

The inherent irrationalism of Pietism is the worst possible response to those great-grandchildren of the Enlightenment and Protestant rebellion against tradition, who reject the teachings of Christianity. If all Christians can do is to help people feel better, so can secular psychologists. If all Christians can do is add pious interpretations to life and a spiritual dimension, so can Hindu gurus and New Age prophets. If all Christians can do is imitate the worst of the world and become "Christian feminists" or "Christian homosexuals," or advocate "Christian abortion rights," then they might as well drop the Christian label altogether and join in the headlong stampede to a gender neutral oblivion. If all Christians can do is come up with pious platitudes, so can the makers of fortune cookies. Pietistic Christianity is the "spent force" Nisbet refers to, not Christianity itself. Pietism and Christianized secularism are not remotely related to the robust philosophy and political economy that true Christian tradition created.

Truth Betrayed

The Christian who abandons the hard edges of the historic faith and its orthodox tradition of reality and Truth in favor of a more comfortable, respectable, sheltered Pietism has abandoned the great eternal witness of the universe for just another religion, another form of psychological counseling to make him or her feel better.

To the extent that much experiential Christianity, pietism, and the like appear to be out of sync with reality, they mirror a drug-like spiritual high that is fundamentally anti-reality. This is orgasmic spirituality for experience's sake, not the love of the Truth of the kind that changes lives and produces results.

To the extent that churches are pietistic, they will reject, or at least be uncomfortable with, art and science, not to mention real people! Art and science ask hard questions; real people are not all respectable. Art and science address complex problems; genuine people behave in unrespectable ways that often raise perplexing questions. Pietists, like all tribalists, long for cultic simplicity and easy solutions: lists of dos and don'ts; radio programs or shamans that tell them how to do everything from having a happy marriage, to happy children, to a happy church group, to a happy retirement. The original, true, odd, creative person in such a context is a nuisance regarded with suspicion.

Pietism invents far more rules for itself than God ever mandated. Because freedom is sometimes frightening, the pietists make their circle of life smaller, not bigger, with every successive generation. Thus life becomes narrow, ugly, strange, and cultic and ends in a rejection of life

---

"If all Christians can do is come up with pious platitudes, so can the makers of fortune cookies."

---

just as the Manichaeans rejected the "flesh." Such narrowness does not reflect well upon Christianity, though perhaps many caught in its web believe in Christ as their Savior. And in that sense they are perhaps saved from Hell in the next life, while they busily create their own sentimental plastic hell in this one. Their salvation has been truncated and stunted in terms of any fruitful, humane, cultural results it could have borne. Thus, cut off from the real world, even real people, pietistic churches have little or no influence in the lives of the people who are creative. The Christian presence in the arts, politics, and the academic disciplines is sadly lacking, perhaps even diminishing.

However ineffectual the middle-class church is, it is nevertheless always attentive to the outward trappings of respectability. It wants its members to be clean, wholesome, to use only "good" language, to be predictable and comfortable. Yet, even as we middle-class Christians have become experts at maintaining our respectability, we have forgotten true virtue. An extreme example of this can be found in the instance of one evangelical pastor I know of who urged his daughter—even forced her—to have an abortion to save him from the *disgrace* of having an "unwed mother" for a daughter. The mind boggles at the contradiction implied by a man who would murder his grandchild to safeguard his standing in a church. Sadly, this example is not fictitious or unique, nor is the middle-class addiction to respectability in the church only limited to such dramatic extremes. (See Epilogue: The Misunderstood Medium—Why the Church Hates the Movies.) If you don't fit in, look, taste, smell, act like a middle-class Christian, you will not find much of a welcome in a great churches today as an artist or a human being. The one thing the middle-class evangelical-fundamentalist church will not forgive is embarrassment.

Given Douglas MacArthur's historic opportunity in Japan, the pietists of today would merely have held religious pep rallies, taught people Bible verses by rote, and preached platitudes or tried to "redistribute" the little wealth that remained to achieve "justice." There would have been no historic-cultural-political-economic vision, no rebirth, no renaissance in Japan under such sterile tutelage. The average graduate from an evangelical-fundamentalist Bible school will, sadly, never be confused with a MacArthur (that eccentric, sometimes vulgar, titan of "Byzantine" virtue striding into the twentieth century, brimming with Western self-confidence, well-read, informed, opinionated, caustic, and emboldened by a sense of the power of the Truth) nor will the well intentioned Roman Catholic leftist who ignores the lessons of history in favor of experiencing an "identity with the poor."

The Truth is like a rock—you either are willing to break yourself on it or it will crush you, because we do live in an orderly, cause-and-effect universe. The Truth is not only "spiritual" but has to do with history, economics, and nations. Pietism lacks the courage to cast itself on the rock and yet is afraid of being crushed. It, therefore, hides within itself and within many churches. Thus, Christian truth begins to take on the trappings of a superstitious talisman unrelated to the actual human condition, sin, or salvation.

9

FREEDOM—SANITY

I am the way, the truth, and the life.

JOHN 14:6

For Christians, the adoption of a worldview based on the concept of Truth results in freedom from false guilt and other dreadful burdens.

The first freedom is the freedom to be *normal*. The follower of the Truth need not be a guilt-ridden weirdo, part of some small, separated band of desperate Christian flagellants seeking personal holiness and spirituality by abandoning life.

To the believer in Truth, the *normal* everyday events of life are received as sacramental gifts from God, not in some odd "spiritual" sense, but directly, literally. The normal relationships of life are sustained. Husbands, wives, children, friends (Christians and non-Christians alike), co-workers, and our other friends who have died, now in the cloud of witnesses, authors, statesmen, composers, beggars, saints, painters, and poets all stand together before our God. We share in one historic reality—one sacramental life lived as an act of worship before God.

The follower of Truth does not need a relationship with a sect or cultic body of believers to be sanctified. He does not need to attach himself to some fleece-the-flock ministry led by some evangelical or "charasmatic" Christian "leader" or "spiritual counselor" who is on a quest for personal power and acts as if he or she had special, extra-biblical revelations for the flock. To the follower of the Truth, the glory of life is *in* life, in thankfulness to the Creator, in a simple childlike relationship to Christ, his Lord and Savior.

His work, his obedience to Christ's teaching, his art, his family, his love of nature and science, his love of the historic Orthodox church, worship, and the Eucharist—these are simple, straightforward, *outward-looking* realities that give joy to the believer in Truth. Few of us, certainly *not I*, have achieved this ideal state. But it is what we struggle for with the inner hope the Holy Spirit gives us as we seek salvation by struggling against sin and journeying toward God by imitating Jesus.

The follower of the Truth is not mired in inward-looking self-analysis. The believer in Truth can be at peace in his vegetable garden tending his tomato plants, savoring a glass of wine, or writing a screenplay, and need not worry as to whether there is some more "spiritual" way that he should be spending his time. He is free to lie in the arms of his beloved wife and revel in all the senses of sexual intimacy and arousal without any guilty sense that there are activities that are more "Christian" than making love to her.

The follower of Truth is free to seek quality and integrity in the music he or she enjoys. He does not need to confuse the mandatory "god-words" of Pietism with Truth. He can listen to Mozart instead of the Christianism of so-called contemporary "Christian music"—usually nothing more than warmed over, second-rate "pop" music. He can appreciate the music of both Bach and the old Mothers of Invention, each for what it is. He can be free to use his mind and senses to sort through what he hears, as regards its truth and beauty. He can appreciate the artisitic merit even in an art work whose reflections on reality differ with his own.

The follower of the Truth is free to apply *one standard* to all things, to all reality: that is, to simply ask, "Is it true?" "Is it false?" "Is it good?" "Is it bad?" "Does it work?" "Is it excellent?" "Is it mediocre?"

The follower of Truth has no strange, weird, or wonderful, special, magical, or spiritual standard by which to judge life, the arts, beauty, and people. Such a follower does not need some special spiritual counselor to give him words of knowledge. The practical, straightforward, unvarnished teaching of Christ, as carried on within the tradition of the historic church, is more than sufficient.

The follower of Truth need not be a strange, mystic oddity. He is a flesh-and-blood person—a real person who may curse when he hits his thumb while adding an extension to his kitchen, but does not blaspheme by saying "Praise the Lord," unless he means it.

He does not need to dress up an argument with out-of-context Bible verses. He deals in the plain currencies of truth and common sense. He lets his yes be yes and his no, no. If Western democratic capitalism, for instance, produces prosperity and freedom, the follower of the Truth does not need to scavenge the Bible for support of his thesis in favor of free markets. Economics, too, is a creation of God through man. Prosperity and well-fed children are good ends to seek in themselves. A society that allows entrepreneurial freedom, allows choice of professions, allows people to use their minds and talents to create spiritual and material wealth for themselves and their families does not need to be theologically justified beyond ordinary, logical, humane arguments. We

"The follower of Truth need not be a strange, mystic oddity. He is a flesh-and-blood person—a real person who may curse when he hits his thumb while adding an extension to his kitchen, but does not blaspheme by saying 'Praise the Lord,' unless he means it."

can discuss the pros and cons of all questions as *already* part of the total reality that comes from God.

The believer in Truth is free to state his case on the basis of its merits. There may be "new" and "old math," but there is no "Christian math." Math itself is already God's. Reality, logic, progress, what works—these things are not the enemy of historic Christian faith. Reality needs no pious overlay to redeem it.

Sanity

The follower of Truth is free to be sane. He can simply say, "I got a job as a farmhand because I needed the money." He does not have to take God's name in vain and say, "The Lord led me to become a farmhand."

He can give good, common sense advice to his friends; he need not indulge in well-meant lies and presumptuously tell them that "the Lord laid thus and so on my heart to tell you."

The follower of Truth can begin a letter with "Dear friend . . . How are you?" He needn't pretend he is writing an epistle to the church at Corinth and open a letter with "Greeting, Brother! In the name of our Lord Jesus Christ, can you send me your recipe for Tortellini al Pesto?"

He understands that reality—the ordinary, the simple, the straight-forward—*is* God's. He does not have to be a spiritual lunatic caught in some permanent spasm of sneezing out pious phlegm.

When those who reject Jesus look at those who say they follow Him, it is not necessary for them to see people who appear to be de-ranged. What they should see are truly *normal* people: husbands of one wife, of good repute; wives who love their husbands; couples who love their children; people who dare to tell the unpopular truth about the true evils (like abortion on demand) confronting our society; people who treasure nature and creation; people who love art and beauty; open people; people who will fight for what is right and against evil at cost to themselves; people who are easily accessible; people who do not speak in some private, blasphemous, "Spirit-filled" code of "God-told-me-so" and "thus says the Lord" babblings; and above all, people who are not divorced from the best of Christian historic tradition but who practice their Christian worship within the context of the historic Apostolic church rather than in the selfish, narcissistic, subjective, and experiential Protestant free-for-all that has done so much to destroy the witness of the church in our day.

Truth is not madness. However, Pietism finally leads to a type of insanity, a split personality in which reality, carved into incompatible parts, is believed to be at war with itself—a madness of guilt-ridden people trying to out-do each other in their pietistic exhibitionism, people who *directly disobey* Christ's instruction to *not* parade one's spiritual life in public like a circus act (Matthew 6:16–18). Pietistic evangelical-ism, fundamentalism, and Catholicism, Left and Right, charismatic and Reformed, have often turned Christianity into a sideshow. It it no wonder that this looks crazy to the world at large. It is.

Jesus

Jesus *is* a historical figure. He is God become man. Jesus' teaching and the laws of God are basic, common sense instructions to ordinary people that, if believed and obeyed, produce life now and eternally.

We believe in Jesus because He is a real figure in history who came from God to save us from the self-destruction and the folly of having thrown out our instruction booklet, our owners' manuals. We can test His teachings against the evidence of the real world. We can look at

> **"The follower of Truth . . . can give good, common sense advice to his friends; he need not indulge in well-meant lies and presumptuously tell them that 'the Lord laid thus and so on my heart to tell you.'"**

what people's lives look like who *truly* obey God and, conversely, at the lives of those who have deliberately departed from God. Jesus came to us to give us a second chance. Through His life, death, and resurrection, He enables us to enter into the favor of our artist, maker-creator God.

Jesus does not occupy some strange spiritual dimension. He is alive in a real place we call Heaven. There, He is building and designing yet another creation, perhaps even inventing a new spectrum, new colors, new biological species, new atomic structures. He is also building a city, a *real* place with measurable dimensions. The fact that the mystery of God and the fact that God stands outside of created time and space makes Him no less real.

God does love us, as evidenced by the fact that He didn't just trade us in for newer models that work better. Instead, the Jewish authors of the Bible inspired by God, the prophets, and finally His Son—God made flesh—were sent to show us the way back, to repair us, to reissue the lost instructions, and, in the case of Jesus, to suffer death for us that death might be trampled by death.

Because flesh, blood, and reality are part of God's creation, His Son worked through flesh, blood, and suffering to reach out to us. God gave us a second chance through a Jewish girl called Mary—a real girl who endured all the physical ramifications of pregnancy.

Reality, flesh, blood, tears, amniotic fluid, suffering: this is the stuff of Mary's motherhood and of Christ's life. The stuff of Jesus' travail. If Mary had had an abortion, then Jesus would have died. There would have been no Savior of the world. There was only one fetus that was the Christ. He was a real baby like you and I once were. He was, and is, irreplaceable. Truth is very untheoretical. Truth is truth. Truth brings eucharistic freedom to human beings, not spiritual chains.

There is no actual battle between "sacred" and "secular." There is one God, one truth, one world. As Alexander Schmemann (former Professor of liturgical theology at St. Vladimir's Orthodox Seminary) has written, "All that exists is God's gift to man, and it all exists to make God known to man, to make man's life communion with God" (*For the Life of the World* [Crestwood, New York: St. Vladimir's Seminary Press, 1963], 14).

God is not an ice cream parlor. There are not thirty-one flavors. *There is only one way to God,* and that is through His Son, Jesus of Nazareth. Other "ways of salvation" and other religions are false. However unfashionable it is in our inclusive, egalitarian age to believe in *exclusive* Truth, Jesus is just that—unique, exclusive, not *a* way but *the* way to God. There are not numerous covenants, but only one, and it comes to us through the Jews. Jesus loves us; He will feed us with genuine pearls—pearls that can turn sham people, hollow men, into full human beings.

10

THE CHALLENGE TO THOSE OF US IN THE ARTS

Feminist literary critics, starting out in the conviction that
women writers had long suffered at the hands of male critics,
have ended up fostering an image of women at least
as insulting as any they set out to protest.

PETER SHAW, *The War Against the Intellect*

I have argued in this book that propaganda makes bad art. Yet today we see that the nearly complete politicization of art and culture is well under way. Pre-twentieth-century art and literature are being reinterpreted through new ideologically motivated political methods by deconstructionists, feminists, Marxists, and others. New works are being produced as mere political tracts, old works obliterated by ideological "creativity." As noted before, political views will sometimes manifest themselves in an artist's work. Yet there is a vast difference between the political or religious-moral views of an artist emerging naturally at times, along with a host of ordinary human and transcendent themes, and the drum-beating "artistic" moralizing to which we have become accustomed today.

The Problem

In the *Selected Letters* of Vladimir Nabokov (New York: Harcourt Brace Jovanovich, 1989), he addresses the problem of moralizing through art. "I never meant to deny the moral impact of art which is certainly inherent in every genuine work of art. What I do deny and am prepared to fight to the last drop of ink is the deliberate moralizing which to me kills every vestige of art in a work, however skillfully written" (p. 38).

Implicit in Nabokov's words is the sense of his own struggle to establish a balance between the temptation to propagandize and the honesty inherently necessary to real art. Today in many quarters this struggle has been abandoned in favor of accepting crude proselytizing as a form of art.

The idea of art being an expression of eternal, common, ageless, human themes is being lost. Therefore, art is being lost, pounded to death by the new political-"religious" moralizers. Even those who one might suppose are equipped to judge the shortcomings of current artworks (produced along party ideological lines) often do not speak up for fear of appearing to be unfashionably out-of-step with the "right-thinking," anti-Western majority in academic and media circles.

Christians who know better have also shown cowardice in the face of a strident fundamentalist and/or pietistic or leftist Catholic juggernaut within the church. Academics in universities have shown similar cowardice in response to the fashions of "third-worldism," feminism, deconstructionism, and pressure to self-censor their opinions so that they are sufficiently "sensitive" to racial, gender, or "sexual preference" questions. As a result, we now have supremely mediocre art and literature being taken seriously, even taught to students. *The Color Purple* is said to be required reading more often than Shakespeare in many college literature courses today! Art and literature are embraced or rejected nowadays because of "politically correct" "right thinking," instead of aesthetic, creative, or historic qualities. For instance, Alice Walker's novel *The Temple of My Familiar* can hardly be considered great literature on its merits. It can only be understood to be "literature" if it is read as the feminist, black, lesbian "religious" tract that it is. It is such a bad book that its publication and acclaim seem to be motivated by some kind of literary affirmative action that has replaced old-fashioned ideas of quality and aesthetic merit. The "Christian" world is no better. In the world of evangelical writing, one can hardly conceive of some new best-selling "Christian novels" like *This Present Darkness* finding as wide an audience as they have, except for the fact that they have propaganda value appreciated by many semi-literate, evangelical Christians who have not read a work of fiction since *Little Women.*

Carol Iannone states the parameters of the problem in the "secular" community very well in an article, "A Turning of the Critical Tide?"

A major strategy in the current assault on the integrity of art from within the literary world has been the denial of the possibility of transcendence. Any claim that a writer can speak beyond his particular historical experience as lived by all men is considered spurious. What

---

"The idea of art being an expression of eternal, common, ageless, human themes is being lost. Therefore, art is being lost, pounded to death by the new political-'religious' moralizers."

---

has been seen as the universal truth in literature, we are told, is nothing more than the disguised or unexamined assumptions of the ruling class, sex, or race.

In no way have those making such accusations actually proved them. Do blacks, for example, find unrecognizable the mournful despair of the Trojan people at the death of Hector? Are women incapable of appreciating the restless dissatisfaction that drives Ishmael to join a whaling expedition? Is it beyond the capacity of a person born into the working class to fathom the overreaching ambitions of Macbeth? Of course not—in fact, such suggestions are *truly* "racist," "sexist," and "classist."

Yet the notion that all literature [and art] is ideological has enabled its purveyors to clear the way for their own authentically political [and theological] approaches, entirely relieved of the burden of aesthetic justification. A whole academic/intellectual industry is now thriving on the infusion of politics into literature [and art], much as some people claim whole industries thrive on the manufacture of chemicals that pollute the environment and contaminate the food supply. (*Commentary*, July 1988)

The "pollution" Iannone writes of has affected every area of the arts.

The Challenge

Yet this is not the first time in history that the arts have been polluted by those who abused them as a means of political-theological warfare carried on by other means.

After the High Renaissance, seventeenth- and eighteenth-century art in most of Europe drifted toward pompous political and "religious" propaganda. In the age of supreme papal power, the sometimes reactionary Counter-Reformation (or Catholic Reformation), and later the "Age of Reason," art was used as a tool for combating "wrong thinking" (in the case of the Counter Reformation, Protestantism) and promoting "right thinking" (in the case of eighteenth-century France, revolutionary leftist ideology). Gone was the sublime transcendence of the Renaissance or the earlier innocence of the High Middle Ages. Gone was the supreme light and innocence of Byzantine art as represented by the transcendent, beautiful, and human mosaics of Ravenna. In their place, painters, sculptors, and architects served to promote a threatened papacy, monarchists of all stripes, and finally, antimonarchist revolution. The florid, overwrought sentimentality of Bernini replaced Michelangelo's purity and truth. The ridiculous, pretentious monstrosities of Rubens stand in contrast to the tranquil luminosity of Botticelli. The beautifully rendered political tracts, masquerading as painting, of Jacques-Louis David contrast sharply with the humanitarian and universal symbols chosen by the artists of Ravenna.

Yet in Holland, in the midst of pretentious propagandistic seventeenth-century Europe, a very different breed of artist worked in opposition to the corruption of art. All was not lost. Holland's mercantile class continued to support painting, as it had since the early Renaissance. The elevated rhetoric of aristocratic propaganda via art had no allure for these educated, hard-working free people. In the tranquil work of painters like Jan Vermeer, Jan Steen, and Rembrandt, we see the true spiritual descendants of the Italian Renaissance, the High Middle Ages, and Byzantium.

Eighteenth-century French painters such as Jacques-Louis David used art to serve political and "revolutionary" causes. In the nineteenth century, artists such as Eugène Delacroix and Ingres also politicized what they were painting. Yet other artists began to rebel against the straitjacket of nineteenth-century academic style and rigid "correct" political content. The impressionists, led by painters such as Manet, Monet, Degas, Renoir, Mary Cassatt, James Abot, and Turner, rediscovered freedom of expression, aesthetic imperatives, and transcendent *human*

"We must produce, or at least work toward producing, works of transcendence in an age that no longer believes that this is possible—an age that has become *fundamentally* anti-Western, anti-heroic, and anti-human—thus anti-art."

---

and natural meanings in their work. Painting was saved from the frozen sterility of politics at least in their time.

In our own day, we face a similar situation to that of the seventeenth-, eighteenth-, and nineteenth-century artists—we are surrounded by reactionaries. This time they come disguised as feminist literary critics, fundamentalist "Christians," leftists, Green party "ecologists," black rights ideologues, liberation theologians, and many more of the people who inhabit the fever swamp of tribal politics. But their intent to misuse the arts and humanities is the same as that of the authoritarian manipulators of other times. The philosophical-artistic answer to them must be the same as that presented by the Dutch painters of the seventeenth century and the impressionists of the nineteenth and early twentieth centuries. They, through their work, produced a poignant rebuke to the idea that art was only for princes, revolutionaries, academics, or conquerors. The everyday scenes of Dutch and French life were infused by the light of transcendent, humane aspirations by these artists *in spite of* the received wisdom of the European elite of the day.

Now we in our own time must stand firm. We must battle against the anti-Western politicization of art, even when it is carried forward under the banner of the lofty ideals of racial, cultural, and sexual "diversity" and "sensitivity." We must produce, or at least work toward producing, works of transcendence in an age that no longer believes that this is possible—an age that has become *fundamentally* anti-Western, anti-heroic, and anti-human—thus anti-art.

Robert Nisbet writes: "Only, it seems evident from the historical record, in the context of a true culture in which at the core is a deep and wide sense of the *sacred* are we likely to regain the vital conditions of progress itself [and] of faith in progress, past, present, and future" (*History of the Idea of Progress* [New York: Basic Books, 1980], 357).

As the woefully mediocre careers of the new secular ideologues, such as Alice Walker or Oliver Stone, remind us of the limits of ideology, Christians who *do* believe in the sacred must carry on, as did the Dutch seventeenth-century painters. As did the impressionists of the late nineteenth and early twentieth centuries, we must *rebel* against the ideological-artistic conventions of our times. We must defend art and the humanities even if we become outcasts for our pains and are ridiculed or ignored by the people who are for the time being the official keepers of the cultural flame.

However, we are not without allies. Just as Donatello and Michelangelo drew inspiration from the Roman ancients, we too may look back in order to learn again how to go forward. We have our heroes to emulate. We can, for example, study the creative spirit that animated the Byzantine empire or the Florentine Renaissance, Dutch seventeenth-century painting, and English seventeenth-century drama. We can reject today's destruction of the humanities by the professional critics with their puny political agendas. Such inspiration, as we find in our rich past, will provide the direction for the long trek home that lies before those who would uphold artistic, moral, and humane standards in a world where, increasingly, the only "absolute" is: "Thou shall have no absolutes."

President of Czechoslovakia and playwright Vaclav Havel, in his remarkable 1990 New Year's address to the Czechoslovak people, said the following:

The worst thing is that we are living in a decayed moral environment. We have become morally ill, because we have become accustomed to saying one thing and thinking another. We have learned not to believe in anything, not to care about one another and only to look after ourselves. Notions such as love, friendship, compassion, humility and forgiveness have lost their depth and dimension, and for many of us they represent merely some kind of psychological idiosyncrasy, or appear as some kind of stray relic from times past. (*Newsweek* [June 15, 1990], 42)

He was speaking of the state of Czechoslovakia, long dominated by anti-Christian materialistic communist ideology. But his remarks could equally apply to our own anti-Western contemporaries who no longer look for transcendent themes in art or believe in virtue, heroism, or even in the rationality of language itself. They risk dragging us all into a poisonous sea of terminal uncertainty.

Beautiful Things

In ancient Greece, the Athenians decorated the Parthenon with the sculpted story of the Lapiths' battle with the centaurs. The Lapiths were a peace-loving tribe whose triumph over the war-like centaurs symbolized for the ancients the victory of civilization over barbarity. Later, during the Renaissance, this story was revived by those guiding the reawakening of learning and art. They believed, like the Greeks before them, that they could also conquer the forces of barbarity, ignorance, and chaos.

Today we, like the Lapiths of old, stand facing "centaurs" of politicized art, fundamentalist ignorance, and anti-Western academic bigotry. Churches, liberal and conservative, so often the defenders of culture in times past, have betrayed us, as have the majority of academics. Yet art does reach out and speak, even from the grave, and true Orthodox Christian tradition is still there to offer hope to those with ears to hear. Stripped of the new criticism, literature still can speak to us. Art *is* a universal language and does give us access to transcendent meaning, if we will forget what we *feel* and relearn what we *know*.

Plato, in the *Republic,* states of the arts:

The man who has been properly nurtured in this area will be keenly aware of things which have been neglected, things not beautifully made by art. . . . He will rightly resent them, he will praise beautiful things, rejoice in them, receive them into his soul, be nurtured by them, and become both good and beautiful in character.

To which I add my own humble "Amen."

THE MISUNDERSTOOD MEDIUM: WHY THE CHURCH HATES MOVIES

Someone at Universal Pictures found the best way to promote the film, **The Last Temptation of Christ:** *to leak certain blasphemous portions of the script to conservative Christians. They reacted predictably to the bait.*

CAL THOMAS, *Los Angeles Times Syndicate*

T oday's evangelical Protestant Christians often mistrust and misunderstand visual media. An extreme example of the basic negative attitude toward movies that pervades the little world of evangelical fundamentalism can be found in the publication *Movie Guide: A Biblical Guide to Movies and Entertainment.* This earnest "Biblical" guide "morally" rates the content of movies as follows: acceptable, caution, extreme caution, bad/decadent, evil. Thus, according to *Movie Guide,* the beautiful children's film *The Adventures of Baron Munchhausen* should be approached with *caution.* It finds *The Dream Team,* a romp of a slapstick comedy, morally *bad.* Unbelievably, it advises that Walt Disney's *Peter Pan* be approached with *caution,* and that the luminously beautiful *Dead Poets' Society* is *bad! Parenthood,* a celebration of family life, is also rated as *bad,* as is the ethereal *Field of Dreams. Dances with Wolves* is rated as "evil." Of all the films it considers, the overwhelming majority receive a very negative "moral" rating of which the examples above are a fair sampling. (It would be disingenuous of me if I were not

147

to mention that one of the writers for the *Movie Guide* savagely criticized one of my own movies as "morally evil.")

Such a "rating system" is a perfect metaphor for many pietistic
Christians' sorry record of understanding, let alone enjoyment, of our
contemporary culture. That there are any willing readers of such sancti-
monious absurdity underscores the paranoid and anti-intellectual climate
now dominating parts of the church. That anyone would want his entertainment prescreened and effectively censored for him by such a publication and not feel that his intelligence had been insulted, is an example
of how genuine values have been replaced with lazy middle-American
niceties by many Christians. Pious hypocritical sentimentality has replaced robust virtue. Some Christians look to such guides to provide
them the means to evade the world around them and, I suspect, their
own need to think things through for themselves. In avoiding the arts,
including many movies, some Christians, sadly, cut themselves off from
a great deal of truth and beauty, as well as an ability to communicate the
gospel to the world around them.

A Christian young person, being raised in the atmosphere of cultural
paranoia typified in the censorious *Movie Guide*, is not going to be encouraged to develop an understanding of, or interest in, movies, culture,
or art. Nor is such an unfortunate likely to develop a love of creativity
or artistic expression. No future movie directors need apply for inspiration to the authors of the "Biblical" *Movie Guide* or those of like mind!

To rate hundreds of mildly offensive or stupid movies as *evil* shows
a lack of precise thinking. Abortion clinics are *evil*. Auschwitz and its
gas chambers are *evil*. The television evangelists who have cynically
stolen the widow's mite in the name of the "Lord's work" are *evil*. The
actions of Pol Pot and the Khmer Rouge are *evil*. Saddam Hussein's
destruction of Kuwait is *evil*. There is real evil in the world without
squandering our moral outrage on a movie. With abortion clinics merrily
liquidating one-and-a-half million babies a year in our country, it would
seem wiser to concentrate whatever public firepower Christians have on
shutting these clinics rather than persecuting those who offend our sense
of cinematic propriety. With runaway children being coerced into prostitution in our cities, surely the evangelical-fundamentalist Pharisees who
find time to print trivial "Biblical" ratings of movies, could direct their
pious energies toward issues of greater moment. However, it seems that

some "Christians," having given up on an artistic culture that they have not participated in for decades, are now content to merely throw stones from the sidelines to, as they foolishly imagine, "pressure the system to change." The "system," at least in the case of the movie business, merely ignores such foolishness.

Cal Thomas, the *Los Angeles Times* syndicated columnist, wrote in response to the picketing of Universal Pictures by Christians protesting the distribution of the movie *The Last Temptation of Christ.*

> A strong case can be made that the very ones most vehement in their opposition ought to be held at least partially responsible for helping to create the type of climate that promotes the success of such films.
>
> In addition, the conservative Christian church in the 20th century has deliberately created its own artistic and intellectual subculture, while failing to take advantage of opportunities to use mainstream filmmaking to fulfill its mission.
>
> Instead, I have heard numerous sermons on the "evil" of Holly-wood, and I have heard preachers condemn attendance at movie the-aters. . . . Paul McGuire, an independent filmmaker, says that not only have Christians had no influence in film's 100-year history, "they have actively discouraged those who are artists, filmmakers and dancers from creative expression." (*L. A. Times Syndicate*, August 14, 1989)

Reform

If authentic Christians want to encourage a renaissance in the arts and humanities, then what is needed is an informed, long-term view of history and art, and an intelligent, willing generation of Christians who will make movies and other artworks from *within* the system. Cal Thomas ends his column, "So, my fellow Christians, protest this film if you like, but then how about devoting some energy to fill the vacuum created by your retreat from popular culture."

We need to acknowledge that getting into the film industry, and all other branches of the arts, is a long, slow, *messy* process. Those who would do so must actually love their work in the arts and accept the fact that believing Christian artists will need to work *through the system before* they can acquire the skill and success to incrementally add their own perspective to their work. (Even then they may well be vilified by the keepers of the flame of fundamentalist ignorance who resent success to all but themselves.) To have an informed view of the arts, we Christians have to understand how art, culture, and, in the case of film, Hollywood actually work. We need the patience of St. Mary of Egypt and the perception of St. Isaiah the Solitary. We have to abandon quick, dramatic, evangelistic propaganda in favor of a lifetime of hard, undramatic work. We will have to read, watch, study, and *think*. We will have to go beyond middle-American, post-Victorian niceties and take risks, keep bad company, be criticized from all sides, and be vulnerable. We will also have to abandon the respectability that many Christians, of the "Biblical scorecard" variety, seem to crave above all else.

All of this will be hard and complicated, like the Christian journey itself—a battle. Simplistic lists of "dos" and "don'ts," which attempt to remove the need to struggle through issues, to work and live for Christ in the complicated and often ugly world, should not be labeled as "biblical." Respectability should not be confused with godliness any more than being "born again" should be confused with salvation.

The example of the "Biblical" movie scorecard is only one of many attempts, concerning several areas of life, to reduce the Christian faith to a list of simplistic rules expressed in the religious how-to books, tapes, radio programs, and television programs which have recently multiplied like tumor cells. These pat teachings are simply Christianized imitations of the fashion for irrationality in the nonbelieving world, which is addicted to seeking easy solutions for complex problems and to reducing everything to the lowest common denominator. Any drive around Hollywood, with its well-advertised palmists, psychics, and "spiritual advisers," shows that the secular world, too, looks for instant solutions and easy, false advice. Christians should know better.

More Movies

Because of the level of ignorance about art in general and movies in particular within the evangelical-fundamentalist ghetto and because some Christians' aversion to modern cinema extends to not even seeing an R-rated movie, (!), many movies are ignored—movies that *do* present ideas that are truthful about issues Christians *say* they care about. Consider a few random examples from past films available at your video cassette store.

Fatal Attraction is a "pro-family" movie if there ever was one. The faithful wife, who stays at home to raise her child, is the heroine—a point that was not lost on the many irate feminist reviewers who excoriated the movie, in such publications as the *L. A. Weekly*, for presenting

---

"Simplistic lists of "dos" and 'don'ts,' which attempt to remove the need to struggle through issues, to work and live for Christ in the complicated and often ugly world, should not be labeled as 'biblical.'"

---

such a "traditional" female role in so positive a light. The philandering husband sets a series of events in motion that clearly shows the wages of sin to be death.

In a similar vein, *The War of the Roses*, a hilarious black comedy about divorce, could almost be an essay on the fact that a permanent, one man/one woman marriage for life is the only ideal for human sexual relationships. The movie poignantly shows that divorce is inherently unworkable. There is also a strong subtext in the film exposing the flimsiness of materialism as a basis for life, married or otherwise.

Crimes and Misdemeanors, a Woody Allen film, is a long discourse on the sanctity of life and a search for meaning through God. The Socratic debate contained in the dialogue could have been lifted from a panel discussion between the late Malcolm Muggeridge, C. S. Lewis, and St. Basil the Great.

The Terminator is a movie about the importance of individual heroic action and moral choices in history, and is directly pro-life in its implications concerning the uniqueness of each individual life, as well as antitotalitarian. There is even a dialogue line in the movie condemning the murderous intent of the Terminator as a "retroactive abortion."

Blade Runner has a deeply moral theme concerning the sanctity of human life infusing its text and subplot. It is a denunciation of human engineering on a par with *A Brave New World*.

The movie *River's Edge* reveals more about the results of godless "valve neutral" secularism in the lives of young people—lives lived as if there is no transcendent meaning—than a month of sermons could. It is a virtual documentary on the results of the failure of "liberal" secular education policies and of the "values clarification" approach to moral education that has done so much to eviscerate our culture.

All That Jazz mirrors the book of Ecclesiastes. The movie expresses exactly the sentiments of "vanity, vanity, all is vanity." It is a film that rings true in an uncanny sense in regard to the problems of a creative life. It illustrates the idea that even while we are in life, yet we are in death. While clearly demonstrating the shallow inadequacies of a life lived only for temporal pleasure, it also expresses the poignancy of spiritual longing that is at the heart of even the most profane creative lifestyle.

Wish You Were Here, a serious and wonderfully made film, is about a young girl who chooses to keep her baby instead of having an abortion, as she is urged to do. It is an affirmation of life in spite of overwhelming odds and a touching essay on the vulnerable sexuality of a young person surrounded by the cynicism of older people who are jaded by their failures.

Rain Man expresses tenderness and compassion even for the unwanted and unloved in our society. It is a testimony against the idea that there is such a thing as a life unworthy of being lived. If the "right to die" (read, "right to kill") doctors, parents, and lawyers in Bloomington, Indiana, who starved the unwanted "Baby Doe" to death, had believed what the makers of *Rain Man* believed, Baby Doe would be alive today.

The implications of the story of the original *Dirty Harry* lead us to ask a valid moral question: What is the individual's responsibility to see justice done even in a society in which the criminal justice system has failed? This is the same question posed by Agatha Christie in her novel *Murder on the Orient Express,* in which she writes a mystery story about people taking the law into their own hands when the system of justice fails. It is also a theme that Sir Arthur Conan Doyle explored in a number of his Sherlock Holmes' stories, and it is a repeated biblical theme.

Babette's Feast, one of the best movies of recent memory, actually takes place in a specifically theological context. It portrays a small, declining, nineteenth-century Danish Christian community into which a wonderful, irreverent French refugee woman comes. The story concerns the conflict between small-minded religiosity and the enjoyment of God's world to its fullest. The battleground is a banquet prepared by Babette (the refugee) and the Christians' shocked, ignorant reaction to what they regard as culinary waste and excess. It is a funny, moving, and deeply thought-provoking movie, and, to one as personally familiar with small Christian communities as I am, uncannily accurate as well as sympathetic in its subtleties.

The Boost and *Bright Lights, Big City* are both cautionary tales that warn of the personal cost of drug-taking as a way of life. Both movies follow a young man in a prodigal son-like story. *The Boost* follows an ambitious deal-maker as he ruins his career and marriage because of his drug use and his blind, materialistic ambition. *Bright Lights, Big City* is a similar story, exposing the ruin to which naked ambition and amorality lead. They are contemporary prodigal son parables.

Driving Miss Daisy is a movie that explores the tender qualities of human relationships and shows that they can transcend gender, race, and economic status.

Cinema Paradiso, the creation of the brilliant writer/director Giuseppe Tornatore, is a breathtakingly humane and beautiful film which profoundly explores the meaning of childhood. In it a local Roman Catholic priest and other characters are portrayed as luminous and important people in spite of the humble lives which they live in a small Italian village. Perhaps no recent film has come so close to presenting the warmth and importance of ordinary life from such a clearly Christian redemptive perspective.

The examples briefly mentioned above (and the list could have been much, much longer, especially if I included older film classics, i.e., *Sunset Boulevard*) are not "Christian" movies, any more than a good dinner is a "Christian" dinner. They are not even all "great" movies. However, they are films that reveal their subjects to us in ways that reflect truthfully on issues about which thinking Christians should at least *profess* to be concerned.

It is terribly unfortunate that many Christians needlessly avoid so many interesting movies because of what they call "sexual situations" "profanity," and "violence" which they view as reasons in themselves—no matter what the context—to avoid almost all contemporary films. As a result of such closed-minded, false piety, they cannot enjoy them or benefit from the useful discussions they would generate in families and amongst friends. Nor can they appreciate the God-given creativity of the people who made them. Nor do they take advantage of the many thoughtful allies they have in the entertainment business who are at least raising questions that pinpoint certain realities in our society in a way that directs our attention towards eternal and transcendent themes as, for instance, is clearly the case with a movie like *Blade Runner*.

No real movie is purely a "message movie" in the sense that evangelical pietists often seem to expect. Good movies must work on many levels. What movies "say," if anything, is only a part of the whole filmwork in question. However, there are quite a few movies that do tell the truth about their subjects, yet are unrecognized or, worse, actually vilified as *bad* or *evil* because they do not fit in with the false niceties of language etiquette or the behavioral norms relative to sex and violence which contemporary, feminized, middle-class American evangelicals believe are suitable to express in the arts—norms that owe more to middle America than to understanding of historic Christianity. Christians have enough real cultural enemies without ignoring or attacking their artistic allies, many of whom may not be believing Christians but nevertheless share a worldview often sympathetic to Judeo-Christian beliefs concerning some specific area or problem.

Religion and the Media

This is not to say that Hollywood has been particularly sympathetic to the historic church and its doctrines, or even to Christian people. Michael Medved, movie critic and co-host of P.B.S.'s *Sneak Previews*, wrote concerning Hollywood's often hostile posture toward religion:

> As the world's most visible religious institution, the Roman Catholic Church has become a particularly popular target for contemporary filmmakers. *Agnes of God* offers us the elevating image of young nun Meg Tilly murdering her own baby and attempting to flush the tiny body down the toilet of her convent room. . . .
>
> Protestant pastors suffer the same rough treatment at the hands of Hollywood. . . . Independent feature films like *Pass the Ammo*, *Salvation* and *Riders of the Storm* have savagely satirized greedy and greasy evangelists lusting after sex and money. . . .

In explaining the hostility to our Judeo-Christian heritage that characterizes so many of these films, industry insiders firmly deny any deep-seated anti-religious bias. They insist that moviemakers are merely responding to the beliefs and prejudices of the film-going public. According to this argument, they are merely following the honorable capitalist practice of giving the customers what they want.

There is, however, one gigantic flaw in that line of reasoning: . . . the movies I've mentioned above . . . flopped resoundingly at the box office. . . . (*Imprimis, Hillsdale College, Hillsdale, Michigan, [December 1989, Vol. 18, No. 12]*)

Though Medved does not attempt to analyze *why* there is such hostility toward Christianity in some quarters in Hollywood, the fact is that Christians have often brought much of it down on their own heads. First, by ignoring the medium, we are voluntarily conspicuous by our absence. There is no "plot" to keep Christians out of the film business. And sec-

---

"Because today the visual media is so little understood by Christians, when we have ventured into making movies and television, our work has generally been mediocre and the results propagandistic and poor."

---

ond, Christian misunderstanding of art, culture, and film is so rampant that it would be hard to prove that the seeds of Hollywood's hostility toward what it understands as Christianity is not simply a reciprocation of the hostility many Christians and Christian institutions have shown toward those in the film business for many years. Moreover, those wishing to expose the greed, lust, and malfeasance of some "Christians" in their movies may choose from all too many glaring public examples.

Jim and Tammy

Because today the visual media is so little understood by Christians, when we have ventured into making movies and television, our work has generally been mediocre and the results propagandistic and poor. This is the complete and tragic reversal of the practice enjoyed in former centuries when believing Christians dominated the arts from the establishment of the Byzantine empire almost up to our own day. "Christian" TV has become an object of ridicule in much of the "Christian community" as well as in the larger world, where, for all the claims by TV evangelists that they have seen "millions saved and thousands healed," tens of thousands of individuals have been permanently turned off to Christ by the ridiculous and crass posturing of televised preachers.

P. J. O'Rourke (an entertaining writer published in *Rolling Stone* and *The American Spectator*) paid a visit to the hellish fiasco that was Jim and Tammy Bakker's Heritage USA just before it closed and Jim Bakker was arrested, prosecuted, and sentenced for fraud. For Christians who wonder what the "world" thinks of our efforts to "reach" them, the following excerpt from P. J. O'Rourke's book, *Holidays in Hell,* (New York: Atlantic Press, 1988), should provide some insight.

> My friend Dorothy and I spent a weekend at Heritage USA. . . . The architects must have been touched by the Holy Spirit because they were definitely speaking the language of design in tongues when they did this. At one end there's the Heritage Grand Hotel—Georgian on steroids, Monticello mated with a Ramada Inn and finished in Wendy's Old Fashioned Hamburgers Gothic. This is attached to a two-hundred-yard stretch of bogus Victorian house fronts, which screen the shopping mall. . . . The Christmas decorations were still up at Heritage. From the entrance gate all the way to the water slide, the place was festooned with Yule lights and other pagan symbols of the season— tinseled evergreens, holly wreaths, snowmen, candy canes. But no Santa Claus. His elves were there, stuffing stockings and wrapping presents, but Santa himself was nowhere to be found. When we walked into the hotel lobby, carolers were singing:
>
>> You'd better not frown,
>> You'd better not cry,
>> You'd better not pout,

I'm telling you why.

Jesus Christ is coming real soon.

While I puzzled over these mysteries Dorothy went shopping. She's normally as good at this as any human female. But she was back in minutes with no bags or packages and a dazed, perplexed expression, like a starved Ethiopian given a piece of wax fruit. What could be the matter?

We went into the bookstore and I found out. There on the shelves were personal affirmations of faith by Roy Rogers and Dale Evans, a born-again diet plan, a transcription of the horrible (though rather un-

---

> **"The problem of crass, tasteless commercialism did not go away with Jim and Tammy. Heritage USA was not an aberration but simply the evangelical, fundamentalist, charismatic norm on a scale of vulgarity that was finally noticed."**

---

imaginative) things you can hear if you play rock-and-roll records backward, and a weighty tome arguing that every time the New Testament says "wine" it really means "grape juice." But I couldn't find anything you'd actually call a book. . . .

Then we went into the music store. It was the same thing. There were racks of tapes and records by Christian pop groups, Christian folk groups, Christian heavy-metal groups, Christian reggae groups, all of them singing original compositions about the Lord. No album was actually titled *I Found God and Lost My Talent,* but I'm sure that was just an oversight. . . .

And that was when it dawned on me. There's only one explanation for Heritage USA. Jim and Tammy were working for the other side. Their own recent behavior seems to make that obvious. And consider the other evidence: a bookstore without books, a record shop without music—what else could these be but the vain and empty works of the devil? (pp. 91–98)

Many a chintzy Roman Catholic trinket shop (not to mention the idle guitar-strumming that passes for a "people's mass") and many of the evangelical and fundamentalist churches in America, their bookstores, schools, and congregations, are miniature "Heritage USAs." The problem of crass, tasteless commercialism did not go away with Jim and Tammy. Heritage USA was not an aberration but simply the evangelical, fundamentalist, charismatic norm on a scale of vulgarity that was finally noticed.

"Christian" TV

Nowhere has Christians' lack of knowledge about art and media or its effect on the culture at large been more appallingly apparent than in our gross misuse of television. Christian TV, as it evolved in the 1970s, became simply televised sermons heavy on fund-raising, with a few mundane talk shows, also heavy on fund-raising, thrown in for good measure.

The unintended comedy of Christian television and its "evangelists" aside, it was left to the so-called secular world to use television creatively. For example, in the 1970s and 1980s, the makers of P.B.S.'s *Nova* series, the *MacNeil-Lehrer News Hour,* the B.B.C's series on Winston Churchill entitled *The Wilderness Years,* the B.B.C.'s Shakespeare's drama series, the anti-television anarchic *Late Night with David Letterman Show*, some of HBO's comedy specials, the second and third seasons of *Saturday Night Live*, and the *Buffalo Bill* series all went to great lengths to expand television's creative possibilities. These shows were mainly the intellectual descendants of American television's one original genius, Ernie Kovaks, or pre-television British theatrical expertise translated for television use by B.B.C. or other British producers. Yet nary a trace of this level of creativity is to be found in that barren wilderness that encompasses the notorious polyester National Religious Broadcasters Association.

Neil Postman writes,

On television, religion, like everything else, is presented, quite simply and without apology, as an entertainment. Everything that makes religion an historic, profound and sacred human activity is stripped away; there is no ritual, no dogma, no tradition, no theology, and above all, no sense of spiritual transcendence. On these shows, the preacher is tops. God comes out as second banana. . . .

I believe I am not mistaken in saying that Christianity is a demanding and serious religion. When it is delivered as easy and amusing, it is another kind of religion altogether. (*Amusing Ourselves to Death*, [New York: Penguin, 1985], 116-124)

The idea that television *must* be used to spread the gospel if the church is to compete in our society is false. The maxims, *If it's there, use it,* or *If it can be done, do it,* should not be the guiding rules of the church. The thriving, growing churches in countries that were until recently dominated by Communism had *no* access to television with which to express their faith or through which to seek new converts. Yet, if anything, the churches behind the once "iron curtain," for instance the Ukrainian Catholics, East German Lutherans, not to mention the Orthodox church in Russia, are faithful and growing faster than many of the churches here in the free West with all our access to the "miracle" of mass communication. Many a self-serving study has been conducted to determine all the "good" Christian TV has done. But who has quantified the irreparable damage it has done to the cause of Christ, let alone the damage done to Christian practice itself now that worship too has been reduced to another component in our entertainment age?

"Christian" Movies

Evangelicals sometimes band together to make a "Christian movie." The result of such propaganda attempts has been the sorry spectacle of pictures like *Born Again* or the nearly endless and expensive absurdity of the "Genesis Project" *Media Bible* in which the makers claim the whole Bible is being filmed. When pastors, churches, and other Christians have tried to back "Christian movies," they have often been preyed upon by has-beens claiming to be "Christian" or "inspirational" or recently converted producers, who descend upon the foolish like vultures smelling rotten flesh. A great deal of money has been spent in the name of "reforming Hollywood," but little film produced. One well-known television preacher in Florida decided to make "Christian movies," so he raised two-hundred fifty thousand dollars, hired a "born again expert" then sat back as the money was spent to no avail and all he got was a three-page "story treatment" for his pains!

The movie business cannot be reformed from the outside any more than the evangelical church. In addition to which, Hollywood is in no more need of "reforming" than many churches are themselves. Having lived in both communities, I can honestly say I have found as much integrity, or as little, in Hollywood as in the wacky evangelical world of radio and TV.

Christians unwilling to do the long-term work from *within* the system fail when they capriciously decide to dabble in film or television for "evangelistic" or political purposes. For a career in the arts and media to be successful, it must be a life work motivated by a love of the medium itself. The movie business is a tough business even for those who understand it and are in it full-time. Imagine the results when the unwary, green, Christian propagandist, however well-intentioned, ventures into it. No wounded cow crossing a piranha-infested river has ever been more vulnerable!

If one wanted to produce a top athletic team of Christians to compete at world-class levels, one would need more than money or a desire to "reclaim sports for Christ." One would need to seek out and then train *generations* of children, young people, and adults to first *enjoy* the sport in question. (For instance, the United States will need years of its children kicking a soccer ball around for *pleasure* before it produces an effective World Cup team.) So it is in the arts and media. When *generations* of believing Christian children and young people grow up appreciating and understanding film and the arts for what they are, and are encouraged to pursue professional careers in artistic mediums *for the love of media, art, and film itself,* then and only then will the presence of believing, informed, and talented Christians be felt in the film industry. You cannot buy nor criticize your way into the arts and media. You can only *work* your way in, *and* you must love what you are doing for its own sake. You cannot see the arts and media as mere propaganda tools to be used for your cause or through which "America will be turned around."

What Is a Good Movie?

The better the movie, then the closer to reality, of its subject and to life as we know it, it will be. A good movie will reflect upon reality in the spirit that Amy Lowell defines as "the desire of a man to express himself, to record the reactions of his personality to the world he lives in" (*Tendencies in Modern American Poetry*, 7).

Science fiction movies like *Blade Runner* or movies about life in small villages, as portrayed in *Jean De Florette, Cinema Paradiso, Le Grand Chemin*, or *La Strada*, may be about very different subjects; nevertheless, all these movies have something in common. They tell the

---

"I have found as much integrity, or as little, in Hollywood as in the wacky evangelical world of radio and TV."

---

truth about their subject matter. For instance, in *Blade Runner* we see the inhuman trends in our pro-abortion, pro-genetic engineering culture projected into the future to their logical conclusion and examined minutely and truthfully from a Christian moral perspective. In *Jean De Florette, Cinema Paradiso, Le Grand Chemin*, and *La Strada*, the villages and country life portrayed ring true to one who, like me, grew up in a small European village where my childhood was spent in and around peasant communities of farm people. The universality and humanity of their stories strike one's heart.

Film Basics

A movie has a story to tell and tells it with pictures, borrowing from painting, words, theater, and music—borrowing from God. There are as many potentially satisfying movies as there are stories, fables, parables, and biographies worth exploring. Movies have a special power over their audiences because they engage more senses simultaneously than most other communication forms. The musical score plays on the emotions. The dialogue can tell the story and develop the characters, involving the audience in an intimate way. The photography—its composition, its movement, and the art direction—shows the audience the highly personal, visual point of view of the director.

Most movies are not "Art" with a capital *A*. Movies belong in neighborhood theaters or at home on one's television, not in museums. Movies are part of the fabric of daily modern life in the same way that theater was part of ordinary life in seventeenth-century England.

The best movies are the ones that achieve their artistic results in ways only available to film. They are not merely plays or paintings on film, but expressions unique to the medium and which take the medium to its limits. *Lawrence of Arabia, Satyricon, The Godfather, Blade Runner, A Clockwork Orange,* and *Citizen Kane*, among others, are movies that tell a story in this uniquely filmic way. In other words, they push reality to limits that only film can reach. For instance, the photographic spectacle and pacing of action in *Lawrence of Arabia* is purely cinematic; it is impossible to conceive of this movie being a play. The devastatingly effective combination of a musical score with the somber photography and close-up performances in *The Godfather* is uniquely filmic in its density. The complex, alternative worlds created by the directors of *Blade Runner* and *A Clockwork Orange* are unthinkable in any other medium but film. The stark narrative use of camera movement developed in *Citizen Kane* is unthinkable in any other medium. In these movies, the atmosphere and art direction, sets, acting, lighting, and sound effects conjure up a totally engrossing imagery and sensory experience. These all achieve what only a film can in a way that a play, painting, or novel cannot. In other words, they all attempt to use the unique qualities of the medium to the fullest extent possible.

Movies are a form of entertainment that, at their most successful, at least border on art. For the time being, I do not believe that there are any movies that clearly can be seen to have the timeless, artistic merit of the art of Byzantium, the high Middle Ages, the Italian Renaissance, or other accomplished periods in our Western history. That is because the medium of film is extremely young, being invented even as we speak. It has not even begun to define itself. A long time must pass before movies can be placed with accurate perspective in a historical context. The Renaissance began with explorations in perspective and proportion by painters like Giotto and Masaccio. Then, several hundred years later, it came to its fruition in the works of Michelangelo, Raphael, and Leonardo da Vinci. Movies, as we know them, are barely seventy years old, hardly a blink of an eye in terms of art history.

Whatever movies are now or will become, to be a moviemaker today is to be part inventor, part vaudevillian, part artist, part promoter, part playwright, part magician, part painter—and all negotiator. Some movies are merely business deals on film, others only extensions of the traditional circus and magic act (nowadays called "special effects"). Movies can be a window on the world and a mirror all at once. The worst movies tell pretentious lies about the kind of world in which we live—either cynical, cruel lies that would twist good and sublime things to show them as frauds, or misleading, optimistic lies that make us "feel good" for no reason. The latter being the kind of mindless pablum that middle America loves and the church often hails as "acceptable family entertainment." The best films challenge and leave us entertained, amused, uncomfortable, sometimes sad, never bored, perhaps angry.

Many "movies" are not even real or complete films. Many are what magazines are to books, what pulp is to great fiction. They exist on film in a technical sense, but they are, like almost all television programs, merely entertainment formulas; they are the cotton candy of the movie industry. They are not evil; they simply exist, just as McDonald's hamburgers exist in a gastronomical limbo. It is a mistake to take the content, such as it is, of these exercises in commerce too seriously. This over-seriousness in judging movies' "morality" often leads people to deplore the state of Hollywood and the moral or intellectual climate of contemporary filmmaking. This is as silly as it would be for the *New York Times* food critic to endlessly review McDonald's various restaurants in the New York area, and then to rant and rave about the decline of cuisine in America. It is foolish to invest a mere money-changing operation with intellectual weight and then criticize it for being less than brilliant! Most "horror," "action," and "science fiction" movies fall into this mundane, often artistically meaningless category. A great deal of evangelical criticism of movies comes from people who are not able to discern between real films and mere deals, people who invariably take things too seriously and give everything an inappropriately serious theological examination. People who cannot even distinguish between bland, often silly, tongue-in-cheek *imitations* of evil, for instance in horror movies, and evil itself are in no position to pronounce judgment on films in general.

Overly ideologically exercised people misunderstand film. Thus it is that the worst film reviews routinely appear in some religious journals and political publications of the Right and Left, for instance the *National Review* and *The Village Voice*. Many political ideologues share, with fundamentalist Christians, an overserious view of film. The Left and Right each have a political "theology" by which they judge the "right thinking" of everything. Like many Christians, those on the Left and Right take everything they do *very* seriously. Thus they imagine that everyone else does, too. They do not realize or believe that most people, including most moviemakers and other artists, are not engaged in some sort of ideological conspiracy, but rather are just earning a living as best they can.

Propaganda—"The Aesthetics of Hysteria"

Ideology often destroys films. The best films are the most carefully made, yet ones where the final result is the *least self-conscious*. The worst films are the most ideologically pretentious. Often this is because their makers have a hidden or overt political or religious agenda. For instance, people like director Oliver Stone (*Platoon, Wall Street, Born on the Fourth of July*, etc.), Billy Graham (an inspired evangelist but an indifferent film producer), and Jane Fonda (of Hanoi and the People's Republic of Santa Monica and L.A., CA) specialize in making politically, socially, or religiously "relevant" propaganda. Their zealous efforts may succeed as a form of preaching but fail as movies. Propaganda is a poor excuse for art or even entertainment!

In the case of Oliver Stone, his efforts to propagandize, in his case from the far Left, have begun to grate on the nerves of people who might even agree with his politics, but, nevertheless, see that he is prostituting his use of film. For instance, David Ansen (*Newsweek's* film critic) in the context of a review of Stone's film, *Born on the Fourth of July* (Oscar nominations notwithstanding), described Stone's politicized drum beating as "his own brand of emotional authoritarianism. . . . Stone is conversant only with the politics of emotionalism. . . . There's no denying that Oliver Stone has a vision; his conviction, his anger, and his talent are for real. . . . But Stone's aesthetics of hysteria can take you only so far; it's the cinematic equivalent of heavy metal, awesome fragments buried in a whole lot of bombast" (*News-*

week, December 25, 1989). As some of Oliver Stone's films illustrate, propaganda is too small a use for film; it is a waste of the medium. The film critic of *The New Yorker* had this to say of *Born on the Fourth of July*, . . . "[The film] is presented in a nostalgic aesthetically reactionary way: . . . The director . . . plays bumper cars with the camera and uses cutting to jam you into the action, and you can't enjoy his uncouthness, because it's put at the service of sanctimony" (January 1990).

Why Make a Movie?

Why breathe? Why procreate? Why eat? Why love? Why pray? Why worship? Human beings have insatiable, God-given desires, and one is the need to create. Thus, a moviemaker is driven to make movies. This creative drive is similar for painters, musicians, writers, dancers, designers—each moved to create by a deeper impulse than merely a rational choice of "career."

Roaming Hollywood, licking the crumbs from the movie industry's table, is an arid business. I have been reduced at times to taking the opportunity to "do lunch" with a prospective producer, not only because there was a chance of getting a job, but because the free lunch itself figured importantly to my nutritional needs in my impoverished condition. For months, feeling like a salesman at a rest stop on an Italian highway—a salesman of stolen watches, the kind that opens his coat to show you fifty or so hanging inside—I have pounded the pavement, tempted in desperation to offer even a casual passerby a selection of moldering scripts.

But I have not been alone; the blind lead the blind in Hollywood. I have arrived at a meeting to pitch an idea and found myself, instead, listening to a producer tell me about *his* idea (a situation truthfully portrayed in the Movie *The Big Picture*). It has dawned on me more than once that the people I have been looking to for help are often in worse career trouble than me. They, under some misapprehension as to my status in the business, have been looking to me for help with their project while I was looking to them for assistance.

Hollywood, that valley in the shadow of ambition, is full of lost souls, each, like some apostle of Robert Schuller, assuming that enough "positive thinking" will induce others to share their secrets of success.

There is as much money made in Hollywood by selling the hope of success, by acting coaches and "managers" for instance, as by success itself. Most hopefuls are mere peons floating in a noxious broth of disappointment, far from the real "powers that be" that run the movie industry, far from the people like superagent Michael Ovitz, who guides the powerful Creative Artists Agency as it packages movie deals for the high and mighty who have "made it."

Occasionally a mere peon like me catches a glimpse of the Ovitzes of the world. Standing in a pay phone on the corner of Sunset and La Cienega, I spot a pale blue Rolls sighing past the intersection. I am tempted to run after it, begging its well-dressed occupant to stop and help me. But reality beckons. The operator wants twenty-five more cents. The parking meter is showing red. The meter maid is only two cars away. "Boy, have we got a deal for you!" Why don't *I* ever hear those words? The Rolls is gone and my party hung up on me. "Your call cannot be completed as dialed; please try again."

Making a movie is like carving Mount Rushmore with your bare hands—an impossible undertaking. All movies are impossible. That is why there are no perfect movies, not even many good ones, and perhaps no great movies at all. There is just too much going on at any one time, too much money pressure, too short a time, too many people with egomaniacal tendencies involved, to do more than paint in broad strokes.

Very few movies are good. Very few directors or actors get an opportunity to choose good material. For many reasons, most directors will never know what they could achieve; they will never have the success necessary to give them the freedom to make what they want. Money and business play a huge part in movie-making, as do egos and greed. When these elements exert themselves like so many powerful currents, it is hard to swim up river. Thus it is, as anyone knows in the film business or in other branches of the arts, a triumph to get *anything* made at all. To even have a job remotely related to your eventual goals in the arts is a victory. To have the necessary control over the various elements to make a good movie is a matter of timing and good fortune as much as talent.

Jesus in Hollywood

Everyone in the arts has their own struggles. Each person has their own story. Mine relates to Hollywood, others' to different places, people, and problems. Yet there are enough similarities between all artistic and spiritual struggles that my own odyssey may have served to be of interest, perhaps even of encouragement, to others.

Hollywood is a desert to me. No scene in *Dune* is more arid. A place of endless meetings with people whose only interest in you is to get something out of you before they discard you. Shakespeare would have understood the agents, producers, and con-men who populate my world.

> Everyone that flatters thee
> Is no friend in misery.
> Words are easy, like the wind;
> Faithful friends are hard to find:
> Every man will be thy friend
> Whilst thou hast wherewith to spend. . . .
> But if Fortune once do frown
> Then farewell his great renown,
> They that fawn'd on him before
> Use his company no more.
> (*The Passionate Pilgrim*, v. 21)

In Hollywood, children are abandoned for careers and spouses discarded for other men or women. In *the business*, friends who are not "making it" are forgotten.

I work with people some of whom seem to believe that they have two lives: one to ruthlessly achieve their career ambitions; the other a mythical life in which living on the prestige and benefits of their career success, they will be human. In these second lives they will raise families, savor life, play with their children, lose weight, love one man or woman forever, and ride off into the sunset. For most of them, their lives are not long enough to be both *successful and human*, let alone holy!

Life in the movie business is an example of what happens when people really do try to "live by bread alone." Since the people I work with in Hollywood are created in God's image, even though they rarely acknowledge it, they have souls. They crave some larger transcendent dimension to life for themselves. But because they will not make commitments to follow God's rules, much less make financial or sexual sacrifices or reorganize their priorities, they naturally gravitate toward easy, pseudospiritual solutions: false, feel-good gods; prophets for profit; gurus; psychics; "New Agers;" psychologists; spiritual counselors;

scientologists; and superspiritual "Christians" of the "charismatic" superchurches—the so-called New Age theologies that Rabbi Harold Kushner, author of *Who Needs God* (New York: Summit Books, 1989), contemptuously dismisses as "religion for impatient, narcissistic souls that infantilizes our relationship with God."

Los Angeles is not a beautiful part of the world. But the physical ugliness of Beverly Hills, Hollywood, Burbank, and the Valley is easy to tolerate compared to the soullessness of many of the human life forms flitting through the Hades that is the movie industry, peopled by men and women with dead eyes. At times I feel myself brutalized and prostituted. I despair of the chance to make the movies *I* want to make. I feel resigned to a fringe existence, making low-budget "B" movies, action movies, horror movies, mindless movies. In fact, these kinds of feature films are all I've had the chance to direct up to now.

I work hard to make the scripts I am given into the best pictures I can. Sometimes it seems I am the only person involved who seems to care about the production. "It's only a little genre movie," or "The foreign market won't be worth more if you spend an extra day in the mix—who cares?"

I am fortunate, one of the lucky few; I have work as a screen-writer and director. That's a beginning. But I have no illusions that my work is *art*. It is merely commerce with some artistic overtones.

Once, long ago it now seems, I thought the only challenge was to "get into" the feature film business. Then I discovered that the greater challenge, once in it, is to be in a position to make a *good* movie, let alone a *successful* one. There are massive obstacles in the way.

"Success at Last!"

I remember back in my more idealistic (read, ignorant!) days living in Hollywood and having a series of meetings with people I thought could help me achieve my career ambitions. At that time I considered it a triumph to get an appointment with anyone *important*—a person sitting at a desk in some dark tower surrounded by the casual trappings of power. How hopeful I was when some such person said they were *interested* in a project I was pitching. How exhilarated I was when they said they *liked* my work!

Once I thought I had had my *big break, the* big break! Steven Bach himself, the man then in charge of production at United Artists, agreed to meet me. I flew into L.A. expectant, *assured,* that I was *on my way.* I sat in an airport hotel room for ten days. Each morning Mr. Bach's secretary informed me that my meeting had been postponed to the next day. The meter was running. That room was becoming a small fissure into which I was pouring money.

Finally, the great day arrived. "Mr. Bach will see you now." Steven Bach was very warm and friendly, gay—in both senses of the word—fashionable, young. He offered me champagne out of a nifty little refrigerator he had in his office. This was the life! He handed me a book, the story of a Dutch art forger. Would I be interested in developing a screenplay out of this? You *bet* I would! A deal with U.A.! I'm here, this is *it!*

Unknown to me, there was a worm in my little apple. At the time U.A. had me writing my script for free, on spec, "we'll do the deal soon," they had another movie in production: *Heaven's Gate,* Michael Cimino's history-making financial fiasco, a boondoggle that would take the whole studio down. My small hopes were, unknown to me at that time, riding on this runaway, uncontrollable disaster being directed by one of the great ego-maniacs of all time. I finished the first draft of my script. I "Fed Exed" it to U.A. Why wait? They need it *now.* I can afford the cost of *"overnighting"* it! Soon I'll have millions! We'll be shooting by autumn! By the spring, the movie will open on a thousand screens! And my percentage of the adjusted gross will be . . .

The next day I waited for the phone to ring. It didn't. So I called. I had Steve's private number, the one that rang on *his* desk—The Desk Of Power!

The phone rang and rang. Finally, an unfamiliar voice answered.

Me: "Steve?"

Voice: "Who dat?"

Me: "Steve?"

Voice: "Who dat?"

Me (annoyed now): "Mr. Bach, please!"

Voice: "He ain't here, he been fired dis mornin', I'se de security guard. I gotta make sure he doan come back 'n' steal scripts 'n' stuff, no one allowed in here dis mornin'."

I had had three long meetings with Steve. I had flown to L.A. twice and once to New York on my own nickel. I had spent at least six hundred dollars on script conference phone calls to various people at U.A.! I had spent three months living off my meager savings, promising my longsuffering wife it was "all going to work out," writing a first script draft, and celebrating my coming and inevitable triumph.

Once during that time of blissful ignorance while I was "working for U.A.," I met with a friend of a friend and ate an overpriced and bad breakfast with him on Sunset Boulevard. This man was a struggling writer-producer. (He now has his own successful network TV show. Some stories have happy endings.) He told me that I would not get into the business until I had "suffered enough." I *had* suffered! What about all the hours of documentaries I made? What about all those meetings I was going to? What about . . . ? I was furious with him.

But he was right; I had *not* suffered enough. It took five years of seemingly endless disappointments, from 1980 until 1985, before I got my first feature off the ground. When released in 1986, my first picture did not do well at all (except in foreign sales, God bless the Japanese!). I had not suffered enough. It was eighteen months before I made my next movie. A project that took me to Africa for ten months. I'm still suffering; I'm not sure it's enough yet! I'm still making "B" movies, and I'm getting a few white hairs in my mustache!

Steven Bach went on to write a best-seller, *Final Cut* (New York: Morrow, 1985), about the *Heaven's Gate* disaster. I'm still in the business; he's selling insurance or something. In the movie business you don't have relationships with companies. Your hopes rise and fall with the executives playing musical chairs between the studios, independent production companies, and oblivion. Your life is no more stable than theirs. You have to suffer.

Since the episode with U.A., I have learned to take constant disappointment in stride. Lost opportunities continue to hurt. Recently I have written a very good script. *The Foreigners* is the best story and screenplay I have authored. It is the sort of project I long to make and would truly represent my philosophy *and* artistic ambitions. It is a story that takes place in Italy during the Second World War. It involves a priest as the hero and a story in which the principal characters wrestle with concepts of justice, civil disobedience, mercy, and redemption. I would, as they say, "kill" to make this picture. Zoetrope Studios, the production company owned by director Francis Ford Copolla, called me. The head

---

"In the end, things boil down to rather simple issues—issues of plain obedience to Christ. . . . And issues of honesty . . . being willing to admit . . . that our talent is limited and that we are who we are, sinners who need to follow the example of Christ in order to succeed at being human, let alone at our 'careers.'"

---

of production, Fred Fuchs (producer of the film *Tucker*), had read the script and loved it. He said that Zoetrope wanted to produce the movie with me directing. He said the script was "brilliant" and the sort of inspirational and uplifting material he wanted to make.

But . . . *But?*

On January 26, 1990 the Zoetrope production company filed for bankruptcy! Only days earlier my lawyer had begun to work on the contract with Zoetrope for my script. Now Zoetrope had had a court judgment against it in regard to ten-year-old debts incurred years earlier on the production of *One From the Heart*. My deal was stalled!

New directors work their way up in the system, making little, often silly pictures, yes even bad movies, or they don't work at all. People like me have to start somewhere. Beggars can't be choosers. Whether other Christians understand this or not, this is what I should be doing while working towards better things to come. If you are a fellow Christian and you stumble across one of my silly little movies and are offended by it, forgive me. Have mercy. Have patience.

Thankfully, there *are* areas I can control better than my bizarre film career. Things such as fighting stingy producers for plane tickets for my wife and children so that we can be together on distant locations, so that I can try to be a good husband and father and not just a movie director scrambling for a living. I *can* bring the brutality and harsh reality of my daily life, when in Hollywood or when doing "deals" or directing, and place them at the feet of Jesus and ask for His Body and Blood to protect me as I take the Eucharist. I can ask my fellow Christians to pray for me. God *does* provide; He *has* provided. The plane tickets have been part of the deals. My wife and children and I are still one family.

Whatever I may *feel* at times, I know I am never alone. There are the fellow travelers, far and few between, who understand the inherent problems and battles of being in the film business. They know what it takes to pay your dues, to suffer in the business, *and* are Christians who will discuss a script *and* pray with me. The people who encourage and lift up, who appear unexpectedly with a light in the dark place and say "this way." There are also the good friends who are not Christians but very decent, intelligent, and thoughtful human beings that stand ready to encourage. God provides such people, knowing that the way is indeed difficult, and we all need encouragement.

The One Thing

In the end, it is not our careers but the ordinary, God-given human institutions of the historic Orthodox Apostolic church, marriage, children, and friends that sustain us. In the end, things boil down to rather simple issues—issues of plain obedience to Christ, simple questions of fidelity to one's spouse and children, of remembering that life goes on in spite of our "career" disappointments. And issues of honesty—of, for instance, not passing the psychological buck for our failures to our parents but being willing to admit our own shortcomings, including the hardest admission of all: that our talent is limited and that we are who we are, sinners who need to follow the example of Christ in order to succeed at being human, let alone at our "careers."

Hardest of all challenges is keeping any "success" we have in perspective. Remembering to consciously fight against the master-of-the-universe syndrome so well-described by Tom Wolfe in his book, *Bonfire of the Vanities*. It is hard to quell the adrenaline that even a modest success sends pumping through our veins, to remember that we are really very limited and that God's time and perspective is geologic in scope—a time reference in which all our huffing and puffing and effort is merely a fleeting whisper, a nod, a blink.

If the disappointments of failure and the sour aftertaste of ego-driven "success" have taught me anything, it is that nothing in this life is entirely what it seems to be and that neither I nor anyone else is dependable or good except by God's grace.

Jesus

Only Jesus is good when everything around us is evil, pale, and decayed, when the very work we do is rotten. It is Jesus who gives us understanding and a reason to live when it comes time to carry our cross, even our small artistic crosses.

When I long for dream producers, like some latter day Lorenzo de' Medici, who might say, "Make the best work of art you can, tell the truth about your subject matter, here's the money, go do it," Jesus understands this longing. He also understands the disappointments that drive us to despair. For He was "tempted even as we are" and His life included a night of weeping in the Garden of Gethsemane.

I fall into gloomy depression at times. There is good reason for despair when you are a human being, a broken machine with a soul, an artist trapped for the time being in a nonaesthetic environment, a faithful spirit dwelling in faithless flesh. Depression is not bad. Jesus despaired; Jesus knows the groaning of a sleepless night. Jesus had His work "re-edited" and has had, throughout history, to endure the misinterpretations of His truth by His supposed friends.

According to tradition, when the young St. Thomas Aquinas visited St. Bonaventura, he asked from what books Bonaventura drew his deep knowledge of God. St. Bonaventura took Thomas Aquinas to the back of his cell and there drew back a curtain, revealing a crucifix on which Christ was depicted in all His suffering. It was from Christ's suffering, Bonaventura explained, that he learned of God, spirituality, and piety.

There is real sorrow, disappointment, and pain in personal setbacks and professional agony, but nevertheless there is hope. Jesus is that hope.

His was a greater suffering than ours. Jesus does not promise prosperity, but He allows us to join our suffering to His. His wounds will hide us even in despair. When my movie deal stalls or fails, when I have no way to tell my side of the story, Jesus hears my pleading.

Jesus knows what we must do to earn a living; He knows the desperate compromises we make in everyday life. He knows the imperfections of our lives. Jesus understands all of life, including the lives of artists.

Jesus is not a pietist. He came to save sinners like me, to save people who are moviemakers, musicians, painters, writers, tax collectors, and Roman soldiers. He came to save people who do real things in the real world for a living, people who are not always nice, people who suffer. Jesus came from death to life.

INDEX

ABOUT THE AUTHOR

F rancis Schaeffer (aka Franky Schaeffer) lives in Massachusetts with his wife and three children. He is a movie director, author, and screenwriter.

In 1974, he produced and directed his first documentary film series, *How Should We Then Live?* The success of this led him to further documentary film work on such projects as the award winning *Whatever Happened to the Human Race?* series (with Dr. C. Everett Koop), which he wrote and directed.

In 1985, Mr. Schaeffer changed careers and began directing full-length feature films. His first feature was *Wired to Kill* (winner of four Golden Scroll Awards from The Academy of Science Fiction, Fantasy and Horror Films, including that of Best Director). To date he has directed four feature films for theatrical, video, or cable release. He is currently engaged in numerous movie production projects and continues his screenwriting, as well as writing, speaking, and teaching as time and opportunity permit.

To receive Franky Schaeffer's free newsletter,
The Christian Activist, *write to: The Christian Activist,*
P.O. Box 740, Mt. Herman, California 95041-0740.

The typeface for the text of this book is *Times Roman*. In 1930, typographer Stanley Morison joined the staff of *The Times* (London) to supervise design of a typeface for the reformatting of this renowned English daily. Morison had overseen type-library reforms at Cambridge University Press in 1925, but this new task would prove a formidable challenge despite a decade of experience in paleography, calligraphy, and typography. *Times New Roman* was credited as coming from Morison's original pencil renderings in the first years of the 1930s, but the typeface went through numerous changes under the scrutiny of a critical committee of dissatisfied *Times* staffers and editors. The resulting typeface, *Times Roman*, has been called the most used, most successful typeface of this century. The design is of enduring value to English and American printers and publishers, who choose the typeface for its readability and economy when run on today's high-speed presses.

Substantive Editing:
Michael Hyatt

Copy Editing:
Susan Kirby

Cover Design:
Steve Diggs & Friends
Nashville, Tennessee

Page Composition:
Xerox Ventura Publisher
Linotronic L-100 Postscript® Imagesetter

Printing and Binding:
Maple-Vail Book Manufacturing Group
York, Pennsylvania

Cover Printing:
Strine Printing Company Inc.
York, Pennsylvania